AF556228

EFFECTIVENESS OF DISTANCE EDUCATION SYSTEM

EFFECTIVENESS OF DISTANCE EDUCATION SYSTEM

Dr. J. Prasanth Kumar
M.A., M.Ed., M.Phil, Ph.D.
A.L. College of Education
Guntur- 522 002
Andhra Pradesh
India

Editor :
Dr. Digumarti Bhaskara Rao
M.Sc., M.A., M.A., M.Ed., Ph.D.
R.V.R. College of Education
D-43, S.V.N. Colony
Guntur-522 006

DISCOVERY PUBLISHING HOUSE
NEW DELHI

Published by :

Discovery Publishing House
4831/24, Ansari Road, Prahlad Street, Darya Ganj,
New Delhi - 110 002 (INDIA)
Phone : 327 9245
Fax. : 91-11-3253475

First Published — 1998

Reprinted-2011

ISBN 81-7141-437-0

Laser Typeset by :

Debug Computer Services
Delhi. Ph. 2438935

Printed at:
Mehra Offset Press
Delhi

PREFACE

The open learning system has been initiated to augment opportunities for higher education and to make it a life long process. The flexibility and innovativeness of open learning system have suited to the diverse requirements of the people and helped in developing the distance education system in a marvelous fashion around the world. In India too, there are a good number of distance education centres and open universities to make the interested pursue higher education staying at their homes itself. Recognising the role of distance education system in educating the people with ease and effect, a study was conducted to identify the effectiveness of distance education system in Andhra Pradesh.

The distance education system in Andhra Pradesh is providing opportunities for the realisation of the objectives of higher education, helping the learners to understand social issues, enabling the clientele to contribute to national development, playing its effective role in the field of women education, able to cater to the students who want mother tongue as a medium of learning, offering a number of courses in various disciplines, and producing and supplying quality study material to the learners. The other side of the coin is suffering from wastage and stagnation, more failures than passes, ineffective student support services, difficulty in acquiring reference books, problem in getting information about examination dates, etc.

This study shall serve as a model to the researchers, academicians and educationists in conducting similar studies at state and national level. The results, discussion and suggestions offered will have their place in distance education system.

At the end, we express our thanks to Dr. K. Jagannadha Rao, Dr. M. Shyam Sundara Rao, Mr. G. Sundara Rao, Dr. T.J. Rajendra Prasad, Dr. M. Vanaja, Director and faculty of School of Distance Education, Andhra University, and Directors and faculty of Dr. B.R. Ambedkar Open University for their co-operation in this research.

Dr. J. Prasanth Kumar

Dr. D. Bhaskara Rao

CONTENTS

ABBREVIATIONS

AU	-	Andhra University
BRAOU	-	Dr. B.R. Ambedkar Open University
DE	-	Distance Education
DES	-	Distance Education System
HE	-	Higher Education
NPE	-	National Policy of Education
OU	-	Open University
PCP	-	Personal Contact Programme
SSS	-	Student Support Services
UGC	-	University Grants Commission
UNESCO	-	United Nations Educational Scientific and Cultural Organization.

The Problem and its Significance

Introduction

Providing proper Higher Education (HE) is of paramount importance to a developing country moving into the twenty-first century. Higher education provides and supplies a wide range of sophisticated manpower needed for the development of a nation. The citizens always look for attainment of individual progress by joining the mainstream system. This is reflected in the aspirations of the people for enrichment of social prestige, achievement of high rate of mobility attainment of economic gains and, improvement of individuals' knowledge and skills over several aspects daily life. While intending to cater to the developmental needs of the society and of individuals, the higher education system aspires for practicing democratic norms. It is expected that the system must be accessible to an optimum level of those citizens who are capable of pursuing higher studies. In this context, the University Education Commission (1948-49) remarks:

> In a well planned educational system opportunities will be provided at every level to the pupils for the exercise of their reflective powers, artistic abilities and practical work. Further, the Commission opined, that our system must provide for every young person, education to the extent that can profit him.

These ideas acted as influential factors in expansion of higher education in the country both through conventional system and Distance Education System (DES).

> Sahu (1985) says that the pressure on higher education has been increasing due to rising social aspirations of the masses. Taking into consideration the factor of increasing rate of enrolment in

higher education, it could be seen that the massive entrance would augment the administrative as well as financial burden on the system. Hence, to avoid increasing administrative and financial burdens, and to maintain academic standards of the formal system, it was thought appropriate to divert the overflow of entrance through creation of alternative channels of higher education.

Moreover, owing to certain inherent limitations, the formal system cannot act as a viable means for higher studies of those who are capable enough to study but belonged tot he regions far away from the institutions, lacked motivation to continue with formal stream, belonged to upper age group, took employment at the end of schooling. found the formal system expensive and discontinued for one or other reasons, and could not take up the opportunity to pursue education as youngsters do etc. These limitations inherent in the formal system paved the way for the encouragement of parallel streams of higher education.

The first clear statement on Distance Education (DE) was in the Education Commission Report (1964-65), where it mentioned ......

> There must also be a method of taking education to the millions who depend upon their own effort to study whenever they can find time to do so. We consider that correspondence or home-study courses provide the right answer for these situations......

Role of Distance Education in Catering to Higher Education

The open learning system has been initiated to augment opportunities for higher education, as an instrument of democratizing education, and to make it a life long process. The flexibility and innovativeness of the open learning system are particularly suited to the diverse requirements of the citizens of our country, including those who had joined the vocational stream.

The Open Universities have also launched a number of relevant programmes in electronics, horticulture, education, computers and communication besides diploma and degree programmes in humanities, commerce and social sciences. The directorates of correspondence education of the conventional universities have also been diversifying the programmes. These institutions are presently offering a large number of diploma and certificate programmes in technical and professional areas.

In a developing country like India, Distance Education is well suited to meet the increasing needs and aspirations of clientele in higher education. As evidence, the Distance Education Institutions (DEI) in India i.e., Open Universities and the Institutes of Distance Education of conventional universities accounted for about 11.5 per cent of the enrolment in higher education in 1989-90. The share and role of Distance Education in catering to higher education is highly significant and is likely to increase in the coming decades.

Concept of Distance Education

The term Distance Education is of recent origin. Teaching and learning by correspondence is the beginning of what is today called Distance Education. Correspondence education is teaching in writing by means of so called self-instructional texts combining the communication of writing. The two constituent elements of correspondence education are the teaching exposition, and the non-continuous communication. The term correspondence education was felt by many to be too narrow and efforts were made to replace it by the new term Distance Education.

Distance Education is a generic term and includes wide variety of teaching, and learning strategies. It is known by a variety of names such as:

(a) Correspondence Education
(b) Home Study
(c) Independent Study
(d) External Study
(e) Off Campus Programme
(f) Open Learning
(g) Open Education
(h) Out Reach
(i) Extra Mural System
(j) Fernstudium (German)
(k) Education a Distancia (Spanish)
(l) Teleducaco (Portuguese)

(m) Tele Enseignement (French).

Distance Education is the name that has been gradually adopted in the United Kingdom, North America, Australia, New Zealand, and other parts of the English speaking world, as well as International Circles. The formal recognition to the term Distance Education was given in 1982 at Vancouver, Canada during the Twelth World Conference of the International Council of Correspondence Education (ICCE). The council changed its name to the International Council for Distance Education (ICDE).

Distance Education has been differently defined by different persons. There is no universally accepted definition.

Holmberg (1977) defines Distance Education as:

> The term Distance Education covers the various forms of study at all levels which are not under the continuous immediate supervision of tutors present with their students in lecture rooms or on the same premises, but which nevertheless, benefit from the planning, guidance and tuition of a tutorial organization.

According to Peters (1973)

> Distance Teaching Education is a method of imparting knowledge, skills and attitudes which is rationalised by the application of division of labour and organizational principles as well as by the extensive use of technical media, especially for the purpose of reproducing high quality teaching material, which makes it possible to instruct great number of students at the same time wherever they live. It is an industrialized form of teaching and learning.

Moore (1973-1977) defines Distance Teaching as:

> Distance Teaching may be defined as the family of instructional methods in which the teaching behaviours are executed apart from the learning behaviours, including those that in a contiguous situation would be performed in the learners presence, so that communication between the teacher and the learner must be facilitated by print, electronic, mechanical or other devices.

The most comprehensive general definition of Distance

Education is that proposed by Keegan (1986). Keegan attempted a synthesis of most of the definitions by identifying the following seven elements of Distance Education.

Quasi-permanent separation of teacher and learner throughout the length of the learning process, this distinguishes it from conventional face to face education.

The influence of an educational organization both in planning and preparation of learning materials and in the provision of Student Support Services (SSS) this distinguishes it from private study and teach yourself programme.

The use of technical media, print, audio, video or computer; to unite teacher and learner and carry the content of the course.

The provision of two-way communication, so that the student may benefit from or even initiate dialogue. The quasi-permanent absence of a learning group throughout the length of the learning [process so that people are usually taught as individuals and not in groups.

The presence of more industrialized features that in conventional oral education.

The privatisation of institutional learning.

The definition of Keegan (1986) indicates the middle ground. Between the extremes of defining Distance Education so narrowly that it becomes an abstraction which does not correspond to existing reality, or defining Distance Education so broadly that it becomes meaningless.

Genesis of Distance Education

The formal education is usually offered in the class rooms of schools, colleges and universities where students and teachers meet regularly at fixed timings. Our usual assumption about education is that there is someone who needs it and there is someone to offer it, but both must regularly meet, if learning and teaching are to take place. But this need not be the only way of imparting education. Knowledge, attitudes, and skills can be effectively imparted without forcing the learner and the teacher to meet in the classroom at fixed hours.

There are ways to effect such an interaction. One of the most practical and effective methods used for this purpose is distance teaching/learning which is popularly called as Distance Education. People often get puzzled at the term Distance Education. Although this term is of recent origin, as a non-conventional and non-formal mode of education, it has been in practice for over 150 years in the form of correspondence education. With the advent of the new and speedier means of communication, the method of imparting education through non-traditional means gained momentum. Correspondence education became possible, thanks to the cheap and reliable postal services.

In 1840, Issac Pittman started using postal tuition to teach persons scattered all over England. Gradually Postal tuition became a recognized mode of teaching various subjects. Thus, the beginning of Distance Education was made with the introduction of correspondence education. The term correspondence education refers to the mode of delivering the learning materials to the learners. Here, print is the only medium of instruction and the printed lessons are the only source of learning.

With the developments in communication and information technologies, various non-print media such as radio, television, telephone, computer, etc., came to be used as instructional media. With these changes, the term correspondence education was felt by many to be too narrow. The search for a new and appropriate term started in the early 1970s and gradually the term correspondence education has been replaced by the term Distance Education.

Distance Education — The Intenational Scene

Distance Education has been developing in a marvelously diverse fashion around the world. This is evidenced by several developments.

- — A large number of individual institutions are coming up to provide Distance Education Courses.
- — Many publicly funded Distance Education Institutions are being set up throughout the world.
- — Legislatures of several Provincial and National Governments are favouring the creation of Distance Teaching institutions.

— Distance Education has been recognized as an integral and valued component of national educational policies.

— The efficiency, validity, reliability, utility and credibility of Distance Education are on the increase.

According to latest information from the International Centre for Distance Education Learning (ICDEL), in 95 countries 779 institutions are offering courses through the Distance mode. This was reported by Sesharatnam (1994) in her thesis.

The names of Regions and the number of Countries and their Distance Education Institutions are given in Table 1.1.

Table 1.1

Names of Regions and the Number of Countries and Distance Education Institutions

Regions	*Number of Countries*	*Number of Institutions*
Africa	34	122
Asia	18	97
Australia	4	66
Middle East	2	3
Europe	18	207
North America	2	217
Caribbean	4	7
Latin America	13	60
	95	779

Source : Sesharatnam C-Ph.D. Thesis, 1994.

The following fields of study in Distance Education Institutions around the world were reported.

1. Broad Multi-subject studies, study skills
2. Agriculture
3. Fisheries
4. Architecture, Building, Surveying, Planning
5. Arts, Humanities, Social Sciences

6. Business, Services, Management, Economics
7. Education, Training
8. Applied Science, Technology
9. Computer Environment
10. Pure Science, Mathematics
11. Medicine, Health, Social Welfare
12. Law, Law Enforcement, Regulations, Standards
13. Personal, Home and Family Affairs.

The International Council for Distance Education (ICDE) has estimated that currently over 10 million students area taking degree courses at a distance, in the world. No organization has yet attempted to estimate the number of people using Distance Education methods for other areas and levels of study. The statistical data in UNESCO Bulletin (1991) shows during 1989-90 about 0.53 million of the 4.8 million students in higher education in India were distance learners and the future trend is likely to be upward.

Distance Education — The Indian Scene

Seven Open Universities in India constitute an important segment of India's DES. The open university system originated in India in 1982 with the establishment of Dr. B.R. Ambedkar Open University (BRAOU) originally known as Andhra Pradesh Open University in Hyderabad. Prior to the founding of BRAOU in 1982, efforts were also made to set up open university at the National level. The first National Open University in India was Indira Gandhi National Open University (IGNOU) and it came into existence by 1985.

BRAOU establishment heralded a new era in the history of Distance Education in India. DES in India consists of two components—Correspondence Education Institutes of Conventional Universities called Distance Education Centres and Open Universities.

There are now more than 35 Distance Education and Seven Open Universities in India i.e., (One National Open University, at Delhi, IGNOU and one each in the states of Andhra Pradesh, Maharashtra, Rajasthan, Bihar, Madhya Pradesh and Karnataka.

The total enrolment in higher education in India during the period (1975-1990) is as follows.

Table 1.2

Total Enrolment in Higher Education in India

Year	*University Departments & Colleges*	*Distance Education (University & Institutions)*	*Total Enrolment*
1975-76	2,426,109	64,210	2,490,319
	(97.4)	(2.6)	(100.0)
1976-77	2,431,563	79,718	2,511,281
	(96.8)	(3.2)	(100.0)
1977-78	2,564,972	119,163	2,684,135
	(95.6)	(4.4)	(100.0)
1978-79	2,618,228	133,459	2,751,687
	(95.1)	(4.9)	(100.0)
1979-80	2,648,579	126,699	2,785,278
	(95.1)	(4.9)	(100.0)
1980-81	2,752,437	166,428	2,918,865
	(94.3)	(5.7)	(100.0)
1981-82	2,952,066	193,691	3,145,757
	(93.8)	(6.2)	(100.0)
1982-83	3,133,093	197,555	3,330,648
	(94.1)	(5.9)	(100.0)
1983-84	3,307,897	N.A.	N.A.
1984-85	3,404,096	N.A.	N.A.
1985-86	3,570,897	355,090	3,925,987
	(91.0)	(9.0)	(100.0)
1986-87	3,681,870	357,791	4,039,661
	(91.1)	(8.9)	(100.0)
1987-88	3,814,417	402,720	4,217,137
	(89.4)	(10.6)	(100.0)
1988-89	3,947,922	454,243	4,402,165
	(89.7)	(10.3)	(100.0)
1989-90	4,246,878	535,512	4,782,390
	(88.8)	(11.2)	(100.0)
Annual Growth Rate of Enrolment			
1975-76 to 1982-83	3.7	17.4	4.2
1982-83 to 1989-90	4.4	15.3	5.3

Source : UNESCO Bulletin, 1993, p. 65.
Figures in the brackets are percentages.

The DES is trying to share the task of providing higher education along with the conventional university system which was mainly vested with the responsibility of providing higher education in India.

Column three, in Table 1.2 shows, total enrolment figures in higher education in India. From column two it can be seen that the share of Distance Education in providing higher education during 1975-76 was 2.6 per cent. By 1989-90, it can be seen that, it has increased to 11.2 per cent. This is enough evidence that those seeking higher education are gradually attracted to DES.

The National trends in the field of higher education in India show, that though Distance Education was started as an alternative channel for providing higher education, it is likely to develop as a parallel system for providing higher education to Indian population.

Of late, it has become debatable whether the conventional system of higher education provided through universities is good or the higher education provided through DES is good. But one thing that has to be acknowledge is that both the systems have a major role in contributing to the goals of higher education in India. In fact, they supplement each other.

Whether the DES is called an alternative channel or parallel stream for providing higher education, the fact to be acknowledged is, that Distance Education approach is attracting more and more learners every year. The Distance Education is a part of the present educational scene in India.

One of the principal objectives of Distance Education is to help people who take up careers to continue their education. The expansion of Distance Education in India during last three decades reveals that the objective is being fulfilled to a great extent.

The demand for higher education has led to a very fast growth of enrolment in universities and colleges. Since, the formal system was unable to meet the rising demand for higher education, DES was developed as an alternative mode at the university stage. From a modest beginning in 1962, when a pilot project was taken up at Delhi University, the Distance Education system at the university level catered to half a million students in 1990-91. The emphasis is also shifting from expanding the formal system to developing DES.

Distance Education — Andhra Pradesh Scene

Currently, in the State of Andhra Pradesh there is one Open University and five Distance Education centres functioning for the provision of higher education along with seven conventional universities. Of them, The School of Distance Education (SDE) of Andhra University, which was established in 1972, is functioning for the last twenty five years. The BRAOU established in 1982, is the oldest Open University in the country and catering to the learners for fifteen years.

The total enrolment of Distance Education students in India for the year 1989-1990 was 5.35 millions out of which the share of Andhra Pradesh was around 82,000.

Region-wise the southern region of India comprising of Andhra Pradesh, Karnataka, Kerala and Tamil Nadu states cater to 61.7 per cent of Distance Education Learners. Though Tamil Nadu is leading in the field of Distance Education in India, the enrolment figures show that the state of Andhra Pradesh ranks second during 1989-90.

With reference to the enrolment in higher education, the share of Distance Education was 21.9 per cent during 1989-90 in Andhra Pradesh. Comparatively in Himachal Pradesh, Delhi and Tamil Nadu States, the share of Distance Education is around 38 percent. Enrolment number wise — Tamil Nadu occupies the first place followed by Andhra Pradesh and Delhi. In India the ranking of Andhra Pradesh in providing Distance Education continues to be at the second or third place.

Clasification of Distance Teaching Institutions

Otto Peters (1971) for the first time attempted a systematic two-fold classification of institutions of Distance Education Teaching at university level by grouping them into Western models and Eastern models. This classification is based on the differences in administration and didactic structures between a study programme based on printed materials plus correspondence or media communication in Western models and printed materials, plus face to face contacts in Eastern models. The basis for Peter's classification are, political structure, and curriculum structure, organisational structure, and didactic structure. E.L. Bushra (1973) identified six categories of correspondence/distance teaching at university level.

Kaye and Rumble (1981) summarized some of the main differences between conventional system and distance learning system.

Neil (1981) distinguished between autonomous distance learning systems and those which operate as distance learning wings of conventional institutions.

Keegan and Rumble (1982) identified seven types of Universities which teach at a distance on the basis of the autonomy of the institutions.

Keegan (1982) developed a simple and useful typology of distance teaching universities on the consideration whether the institutions is established solely for distance teaching or established for both distance and conventional teaching.

Significance of the Study

The clientele to Distance Education stream of higher education in Andhra Pradesh is being catered to by one open university and five directorate attached to the conventional universities. Besides, there are universities like IGNOU, National Open University and Madras, Annamalai, Madurai Kamaraj, Bharathidasan etc., located in Tamil Nadu State which are also attracting clientele from Andhra Pradesh.

The SDE, Andhra University and BRAOU are the oldest Distance Education agencies in the state. The rest of the Distance Education agencies are young and developing. The DSE in Andhra pradesh is in different stages of development. There is increasing enrolment and increased financial inputs into the system. In this context, the role of Distance Education in Andhra Pradesh in achieving the goals of higher education has significance.

Though its current share is 21.9 per cent of the enrolment, a future increase in the share is anticipated. By the end of this decade 30 to 35 per cent of the students in higher education are likely to be distance learners. At this juncture, the DES will become a parallel system for providing higher education.

Currently, six per cent of the Distance Education learners are in the age range of 20 to 25 years. The student profile shows, that it is mainly youth in this age range who is getting attracted to the DES.

The Distance Education stream is also helping in the area of women's education. 38.9 per cent of the Distance Education learners in the country are women. In Andhra Pradesh 33.5 per cent of the Distance Education learners are women.

The role of Distance Education in catering to the goals of higher education is unquestionable. The only question that educationists have to answer is, how best to improve the Distance Education machinery to cater to the changing goals of higher education.

Serious attempts are being made in planning of higher education is conventional universities to make it effective. The last decade has seen vast expansion of higher education through Indian Universities.

In our secular, democratic set up, the document on National Policy of Education 1986 (NPE) has projected the concepts of modernization, value education, social contributions, and vocationalisation.

The Distance Education Universities were started in 1980s, and most of the universities have started Distance Education centres simultaneously. The public have come to realise the place of Distance Education in their lives. There is vast expansion in terms of number of courses, and structural organization of the Distance Education machinery.

A lot of planning has gone into the Indian DES and its rate of expansion and progress appears to be faster than that of a conventional university. The DES has become self-sufficient, well staffed, accessible, and catering to a large number and wide range of clientele.

Quality and Defects of Higher Education in India

Quantitative expansion by itself is not an indication of quality education. The progress has to be planned in both qualitative and quantitative directions. Much is said about the quality and defects of higher education in India. The main defects of Indian higher education are :

(i) Un-even spread and development of higher education.

(ii) Variations in quality of teaching and research due to variation in infra-structural facilities.

(iii) Courses are not related to the job market and environment.

(iv) Erosion in the credibility of evaluation system.

The DES, if it has to properly cater to higher education, has also to take care of these defects and move in the direction of realising the goals of higher education, as projected by The New Education Policy (1986).

The following review of the post-independence education policies in India outline the changing goals of higher education.

The university Education Commission (1948-49), which is the first post-independence Education Commission in India, suggested the following goals of higher education.

1. To teach that life has a meaning.
2. To awaken the innate ability to live the life of soul by developing wisdom.
3. To train for democracy.
4. To train for self-development.
5. To develop certain values like fearlessness of mind, strength of conscience and integrity of purpose.
6. To acquaint with cultural heritage for its regeneration.
7. To enable to know that education is a life long process.
8. To understand the present as well as the past.
9. To impart vocational and professional training.

The Education Commission (1964-66), identified the following goals of higher education.

1. To seek new knowledge, to engage in the pursuit of truth, and to interpret new knowledge in the light of new needs and discoveries.
2. To provide right kind of leadership in all walks of life and cultivating right interests, attitudes, moral, and intellectual values.
3. To provide society with competent men and women, trained in agriculture, arts, medicine, science and technology and other professions.
4. To promote equality and social justice.

5. To faster in the teachers and students, the attitudes and values needed for developing life in individual and society.

The commission also recommended for the provision of time and correspondence courses and extension programmes of various kinds, to provide varied educational facilities.

Based on recommendations of the Education Commission, a resolution on National Policy on Education (NPE) was formally adopted by the parliament in the year 1968. The document highlighted the following aspects related to higher education and correspondence education.

1. The demand for higher education, the college or university department should be determined with reference to the laboratory, Library, other facilities and the strength of the staff.
2. University should be started only when adequate funding has been made for the purpose and care has been taken to ensure proper standards.
3. Special attention should be given towards Post-graduate courses and improvement of standards of training and research.
4. Centres of advances studies should be strengthened.
5. Facilities for part-time education and correspondence courses should be developed on a large scale at the university stage.

The policy frame work of higher education in India issued by the University Grants Commission (U.G.C.) (1976) focussed the following objectives:

1. To incalculate and promote the basic human values.
2. To develop faith and conviction in our cultural heritage and traditions.
3. To develop critical evaluation of political, social, and economic order and co-operativeness to contribute to the social and national cause.
4. To develop leadership in the field of science and technology.
5. We are living in a world of change. The twenty-first century which is waiting, compels us to integrate ourselves into historical process of change, is the demand of the new culture.

The National Policy of Education (1986), which has recognised and speltout the goals of higher education, while pointing out that higher education should be made dynamic, says;

1. To provide people with an opportunity to reflect on the critical, social, economic, cultural, moral, and spiritual issues facing humanity.
2. To contribute to National Development through dissemination of specialised knowledge and skills.
3. To serve as crucial factors for survival.
4. To play a key role in producing teachers for the education system, as higher education is at the apex of educational pyramid.

The main features of the programmes and strategies to impart necessary dynamism to the higher education system consist of the following:

1. Consolidation and expansion of institutions.
2. Development of autonomous colleges and departments.
3. Re-designing the courses.
4. Training of Teachers.
5. Strengthening of research.
6. Improvements in efficiency.
7. Creation of structures for co-ordination at the state and the national level.
8. Mobility

While the growth of higher education through conventional universities has been steady and planned, the growth of higher education in India through Distance Education System is need based and fast developing. By virtue of the fact that Distance Education is attracting more and more students, a quantitative growth of this system in India is to be expected.

The UNESCO (1993) bulletin points out,that an uneven growth of Distance Education in various regions of India is evident.

There is a need to make the DE system effective and, know how effective it is. Mere quantitative expansion of the system cannot be an indicator of the quality of education. To meet the demands of the population for higher education, the DES is showing fast quantitative expansion. When the learners are limited in number, no doubt, the system is effective. But, the pressures of catering to increased number of learners like providing varied courses, providing Student Support Services (SSS), maintaining timely learner contact by using multimedia, evolving high quality Self-Learning Instructional Materials (SLIMS) etc.; are needed to make this system effective. The only, the goals of higher education can be realised, quality improved and, the system can be made effective.

A system is effective, when it is running smoothly. From the view point of the learner the Distance Education system is effective when his entry into Distance Education stream is easy, when the learning system is suitable to him, when the administrative procedures like submitting applications, getting information, writing examinations, and passing out of the stream are well planned, easy and least troublesome.

The system can also be said to be effective when the organizational hierarchy is well defined, and each individual participating in the system has a favourable view of the concept. In the DES this favourable attitude is specially necessary for those at the helm of affairs.

The system can be said to be effective, when the general trends are upward; like enrolment growth, economic growth, curriculum growth, and faculty growth.

Much of the research work in the field of Distance Education has focused its attention on the basic concept, the learner, his profile and needs, and the Students Support Services (SSS). Not many of the investigators have focused proper attention on the area of the effectiveness of DES in realising the goals of higher education. Hence, this area of research in the field of Distance Education was chosen for this study.

Research into this area can influence planning, identification of defects, qualitative improvement of this system, need for restructuring the educational goals to suit the Distance Education learners and identification of the developing trends in the system,. It was felt that by entering into this area of research, useful conclusions on DES can be drawn, research techniques could be developed and this developing system of education in the modern world can be better understood.

Need for the Study

Studies in the area of the Effectiveness of DES in Realising the Goals of Higher Education are needed. Educational research is not undertaken in this area. Sujatha (1988) in her review paper indicated that the studies in Distance Education are:

> Too few, too dispersed and yet too inadequate to derive proper feed back, for planning and management of the system on a scientific basis.

The classification of Sahoo (1991) on the Indian studies in Distance Education also shows that research in this area viz., Effectiveness of Distance Education system in Goal Realisation, is not undertaken by research workers in India.

According to him, the areas covered in the research works on Distance Education are:

1. Instructional processes: Study habits of learners, syllabi, lesson scripts, assignments, personal contact programmes regional study centres, library studies, other means of instruction, evaluation and general management.
2. Teachers: Their involvement in the system.
3. Learners: Their characteristics, their reasons for joining the courses and assignment of needs.
4. Drop-outs.
5. Growth of the system.
6. Attitude/reaction of participants towards the system.
7. Out put; Analysis of achievement.
8. Comparison of achievement of correspondence course students with that of regular course students.
9. Costs: Unit cost, private cost, cost structure, Cost benefits etc.

Most of the studies in Distance Education are of descriptive and qualitative, but not evaluative. There were a few exploratory studies trying to evaluate the system by focussing on one or two aspect at a time. That kind of studies cannot facilitate decision making and system development. Most of the studies concentrated on singly component investigations at the micro level.

Hence, it was felt that the holistic model of investigation to look at the intricate relationships will yield useful knowledge. There is a need to undertake evaluation studies DES taking into account the context of the functioning of the system. The may help in giving directions for innovations in the DES in the Indian context.

Though, we speak of two systems by calling them distance and conventional; it should be remembered that, the learners of both the systems are aiming at higher education. Hence, evaluative studies of DES are as important as evaluative studies of the conventional system.

At the international level, the DES has been so ambitious that, it has developed into Distance Education Universities, also called Open Universities. World wide the number of Open Universities are thirty by the year 1994. In Indian the total number of Open Universities are seven. This itself speaks that Indian people are getting attracted to the open learning system through Distance Education mode. The DES as an alternative channel for providing higher education for Indian masses is an important feature of the current Indian Educational system.

Besides, almost every conventional university is equipped with a Distance Education Centre offering a wide range of courses. The number of Distance Education Centres in India at present are more than thirty-five.

A comparision of the student enrolment in conventional universities and DES shows healthy growth rate in quantitative direction.

In the conventional university, there are controls on student enrolment. Unless proper infrastructure is provided the conventional university will not increase the students intake. The concept of Distance Educations is attracting more and more people to the idea of acquiring qualifications and receiving higher education. The DES does not place restrictions on students intake. Hence, one finds that DWS shows faster growth rate in quantitative direction. The quantitative growth in DES and its parallel growth as an alternative to conventional university education makes it the current area of educational research. There is a need for continuous comprehensive and periodic evaluation of its effectiveness.

The DES has developed a structural and organizational pattern of its own. It awards educational qualifications equated with those awarded by a conventional university. In this context, there will always be a discussion about the quality of education provided through these two systems viz., the Conventional Universities and DES. This leads to the quality of higher education through DES and whether the DES is effective.

The DES in the modern world is considered the educational system of the future. By catering to clientele of different backgrounds and age groups, the system is doing yeoman service to the cause of education at the university level.

The state of Andhra Pradesh has become one of the pioneers and leaders in the field of Distance Education in India. The State Government and the Central Government are the funding agencies of this system. The system is expected to e effective in functioning by catering to the needs of a large and growing number of Distance Learners. Though the student composition of this system is different from that of a conventional university for higher education, research has shown that the Distance Education learner is equally motivated to receive higher education.

Though the routes are different, the ultimate aim is the acquisition of higher education. Evidently, both the systems should function effectively to realise the goals of higher education. It also means that recommendations made for improving the quality of higher education are applicable to both the systems. The recommendations of NPE (1986) for improving the quality of higher education in India, and the areas identified by them for strengthening the system have equal relevance to DES.

From the foregoing observations, it can be asserted, the Distance Education is an important contributory to the system of higher education in India.

As already pointed out, much of the research work in the field of Distance Education is still piecemeal and at consolidation stage. A refocusing of the area if research in this field needs to be attempted, by posing a basic question in terms of the effectiveness of DES in realising the goals of higher education. Hence, this piece of research is attempted with the following question which has education implications to the state of Andhra Pradesh.

Is the Distance Education System in Andhra Pradesh effective to realise the goals of higher education?

Focus of the Study

The concept of Distance Education, its inclusion into the terminology of education has resulted in vast educational literature. A separate system of education, viz., DES has grown out of this concept, heralding the constitution of open universities in the modern world. Educationists have clarified the concept of Distance Education, defined the role of Open Universities, explained the methods of educating Distance learners and, formulated guidelines for the relevant instructional, evaluations, and organizations aspects of this system. In this context of the growth, development, and organization of this concept into the educational system, frequent evaluative studies in terms of its effectiveness for realising educational goals, become relevant.

Evaluative studies in Distance Education can be in terms of a region, nation or nations. To conduct this study viz., effectiveness of Distance Education system of Andhra Pradesh in realising the goals of higher education, descriptive survey method was adopted. Institutional studies with in the system were considered adequate to yield the desired information on the goals of the study.

For the purpose of this study, statistical information on Distance Education was chosen to the extent available. With the help of consolidate statistical data over the years, one can make a detailed trend analysis.

At the same time, statistical data by itself cannot give a comprehensive picture of the educational scene. Personal information gathered form the teacher and taught in an educational system and, on the spot observations of the system will partially complete the picture and, help in answering a research question of this magnitude.

Hence, it was felt desirable to focus the attention by adopting a three-way approach of data gathering viz., Trend analysis, Interviewing teachers, and gathering learner opinion, which will enable in drawing pertinent and useful conclusions. The focus was on the institution as a whole, and on the teachers and learners, in particular.

As already explained, the various institutions of Distance Education in Andhra Pradesh are in different stages of growth and development. But, a study of well established Distance Education institutions in the state can help in drawing conclusions, which are applicable to the growing institutions.

A systematic and well focussed understanding of the growth of two well established institutions, one Open University and the other SDE, can help in answering the research question. The institutions are to be studied in descriptive study approach in terms of growth and development, current status and anticipated future.

Hence, the main focus of this investigation is to draw generalizations about the effectiveness of Distance Education System in Andhra Pradesh by studying and evaluating some well established institutions of the state.

The title of this study is:

"EFFECTIVE OF DISTANCE EDUCATION SYSTEM OF ANDHRA PRADESH IN REALISING THE GOALS OF HIGHER EDUCATION - AN EVALUATIVE STUDY".

Objective of the Study

The main aim of this investigation is to study effectiveness of the present Distance Education system in Andhra Pradesh in realising the goals of higher education. It is proposed to draw conclusions regarding the effectiveness.

A. *Through Institutional Study by Identifying:*

1. Enrolment trends.
2. Economic trends.
3. Growth in infrastructure.
4. Curriculum and course trends.
5. The trend of learners success in the system.
6. Multi-media usage trends.

B. *Through Faculty by:*

1. Identifying the faculty opinions and the goals of higher education that are realized by the Distance Education system.
2. Finding faculty opinions on areas of Distance Education

system that need to be improved and strengthened.

C. *Through Learners by:*

1. Identifying the learner opinion on the goals of higher education that are realised by the Distance Education system.
2. To identify the major learner opinion towards the Distance Education system.
3. Finding learner opinion on areas of Distance Education system that need to be improved and strengthened.

The present study of Distance Education was made with the above objectives in mind.

Limitation of the Study

It is not very easy to evaluate the effectiveness of the present Distance Education system in Andhra Pradesh the goals of higher education realized by it.

While, it is desirable to make a comprehensive study of the total system in the state, this could not be included in the scope of the present study. While there are five Distance Education Centres and one Open University in Andhra Pradesh, the investigator chose one from each category for this diecriptive survey. The chosen two institutions are well established, and hence were considered as indicators of trends in the Distance Education system in Andhra Pradesh.

Attempts were made to make the date objective by adopting different techniques of data gathering i.e., statistical date of the institutions over the years, opinion identification through interview schedule, and use of opinionnaire as a tool. The information so gathered was combined, compared, and evaluation of system effectiveness was attempted.

The sampling included the teachers and taught only. No extra variables were chosen for this study.

The interview sample was restricted to faculty at the senior administrative and policy decision levels. Teaching faculty associated with study centres were not contacted. The sampling technique used for contacting the learners was quota sampling.

The available statistical data from the institutions was analysed and conclusions derived.

2

Review of Related Literature

Introduction

This chapter presents the review of studies conducted so far on Distance Education System of instruction at University stage. Such an attempt is made to develop an overall idea about the nature and findings of the previous studies and to arrive at a rationale for the study. In this context, attempt is made to classify the studies. There is an effort to highlight the methods and procedures adopted in the studies. While doing the review, the studies conducted abroad and in India have been classified separately.

To look into the development of Distance Education System, the problems and issues emerging from them, an attempt is made to review the available studies in the Indian context separately.

Sujatha (1988), in her review paper to the workshop on "Research in Distance Education and Educational Technology" organised by the National Institute of Educational Planning & Administration, New Delhi, indicated that the following nine areas were covered in the research work in Distance Education during the decade 1976-86. They are:

1. *Growth* : System, policies, course structure, level of courses, enrolment and organisation;
2. *Learners* : assessment of needs, their reasons for joining the courses and their characteristics;
3. *Drop-outs* : rate of drop-outs, characteristics of drop-out;
4. *Teachers* : characteristics of teachers, and their involvement in the system;

5. *Instructional Process* : study habits of learners, syllabus, lesson scripts, assignments, Pcps, regional study centres, library studies, other means of instruction, evaluation and general management;
6. Course development and evaluation.
7. *Output* : analysis of achievement, comparision of achievement of correspondence course students with that of regular course students, achievement correlates, and long term impacts;
8. *Costs* : Unit cost, private cost, cost structure, cost benefits etc.;
9. Attitudes/reactions of participants towards the system.

Sahoo made an areawise classification of Indian studies in Distance Education in 1991, as shown in Table 2.3.

Table 2.3

Areawise Classification of Indian Studies in Distance Education

Area of Study	*Conducted by*
1. System's Growth	Dutt (1976), Biswal (1979), Khan (1982), Dutt (1984), Gupta (1985), Sahoo (1985a), Sahoo (1985b), Bala Subramaniam (1986)
2. Learners	Anand (1979), Biswal (1979), Gomathi (1982), Khan (1982), Pillai & Mohan (1983), Sahoo (1985b), Pugazenthi (1985)
3. Dropouts	Balasubramaniam (1976), Biswal (1979), Gupta (1985), Sahoo(1985b), Pugazenthi (1985)
4. Teachers	Biswal (1979), Khan (1982), Sahoo (1985b), Pugazenthi (1985)
5. Instructional Process	Bhusan & Sharma (1976), Anand (1979) Biswal (1979), Mathur (1979), Gomathi (1982), Khan (1982), Pillai & Mohan (1983), Sahoo (1985b), Pugazenthi (1985), Balasubramaniam (1986), Sudame & Pugazenthi (1986)
6. Evaluation Process	Anand (1979), Biswal (1979), Khan (1982), Pillai & Mohan (1983), Sahoo (1985b), Pugazenthi (1985), Balasubramaniam (1976), Sudame Pugazehti (1986)
7. Course Development and Evaluation	Khan (1982), Sarwal (1984), Vydehi (1984)

(*Contd.*)

Area of Study	*Conducted by*
8. Output	Sashi (1972), Anand (1979), Biswal (1979), Panda (1980), Pandey (1980), Gomathi (1982), Pillai & Mohan (1983), Gupta (1985), Sahoo (1985b), Pugazenthi (1985), Reddy (1986)
9. Finance	Dutt (1978), Gupta (1978), Biswal (1979), Pandey (1980), Gupta (1985) Sahoo (1985b), Pugazenthi (1985), Aggarwal (1986), Dutt (1986)
10. Attitude towards whole system	Khan (1982), Sahoo (1985b), Sahoo & Bhat (1985), Rana (1986)

Panda (1992) examined a total of 142 research studies in Distance Education and the breakup is given in Table 2.4.

Studies Abroad

Policies, Pattern and Growth

There have been several attempts on conducting studies on this area, Perry (1976), Sims (1978), Green (1980), Schuyer (1981), are some of them. The common findings that have been marked in these studies are that the organisation structures are integrated within a larger system of education, usually a large university complex. Within each education set up, the systems follow certain overall policy statements on their roles and functions. The systems however, have unique policy making models.

Learners of the System

Characteristics of Learners

Studies concerned with learners' characteristics can be recognised with several background variables like age, sex, marital status, regional background, employment, occupation, social class and academic qualification. Further, in some of the cases analysis of learners' characteristics were done taking into consideration the courses inside the correspondence education system and outside parallel system. With regard to the age of the students, Glatter and Wedell (1971) , McIntosh (1974) found that in the United Kingdom (U.K.) very high percentage of correspondence education students belonged to around thirty years of age. Peters (1965) found that in the United States of America (U.S.A.) and

Table 2.4

Area-wise Resarch Study Categories

Area	*Institutional Projects*		*Private Projects*		*Water's Dissertations*		*M.Phil. Dissertation*		*Doctoral Dissertations*		*Total*
	CE	OU	CE	OU	CE	OU	CE	OU	CE	OU	
Concept, Growth & Development	6	7	19	9	-	1	-	-	1	1	44
Curriculum/Course Planning & Development	-	3	-	-	-	-	-	-	-	-	3
Instruction/Teaching	2	5	2	3	-	-	-	-	2	-	14
Media & Technology	-	2	-	2	-	-	-	-	-	-	4
Learners and Learning	3	4	12	6	3	-	-	-	2	1	31
Institutional Policy Management	2	-	1	-	-	-	-	-	1	-	4
Economics	2	3	5	-	-	-	-	-	3	-	13
Evaluation/Programme Evaluation	2	12	-	3	2	-	2	-	4	-	25
Staff Development	-	1	1	2	-	-	-	-	-	-	4
Total	17	37	40	25	5	1	2	-	13	2	142

CE = Correspondence Education
OU = Open University (Including open school)

West Germany around 55 to 56 per cent correspondence students belonged to thirty years age group.

Glatter and Wedell (1971) further found that with regard to the sex of students of correspondence education in the U.S.A. and the U.K. most of the students i.e., around seventy per cent were men. McIntosh (1974) found that in the cases of Open University, the U.K., the situation of 1971 i.e., seventy per cent men and thirty per cent women, changed towards fifty six per cent men and forty four per cent women by the year 1974.

Regarding marital status of correspondence students, Short 1967, Glatter and Wedell 1971, McIntosh 1974 found that most of them were married and had children.

About residences of students the studies like Peters (1965) and Glatter and Wedell (1971) revealed that in comparision to ruralites more urban based learners were attracted towards correspondence system.

The studies on employment and occupation background of correspondence students by Glatter and Wedell (1971) revealed that among professional course students, ninety nine per cent were employed-ones where as in the case of general courses sixty nine per cent students were having employment.

Glatter and Wedell (1971) further found in general that the employed students were absorbed in several occupations like civil servants, industrial workers, library servants, house wives, commerce and private sector oriented professionals, clerical and office staff, administration and management personnels, shop keepers Armed forces personnels etc.

In another study by Perry (1976), it could be found that during 1971 only thirty three per cent students of the Open University were fulfilling the minimum qualification requirements for entry into other British Universities. However, by the year 1975 the students percentage from such category had increased to a 46.4 per cent.

There were studies by Glatter and Wedell (1971), which focussed on coursewise analysis of correspondence students academic background. It was found that there was no difference between academic background of general and professional course students, summer and non-summer students.

Enrolment of Students

The studies on enrolment in different types of correspondence courses by Glatter and Wedell (1971) revealed different findings. In the U.K. a greater proportion of students were preparing for professional qualifications that for external degrees.

Dropouts

Peters (1965) and Childs (1971) finding regarding rates of dropouts in correspondence system was that their percentages were quite high i.e., Seventy two per cent, in west Germany, Sixty per cent in the U.S.A.

The major reasons for drop outs, as identified by different studies were :

(i) job interference with study.

(ii) lack of time.

(iii) interference with family home responsibilities.

(iv) changes in career plans.

(v) problems with the modes of studies and completion of lessons.

(vi) late submission of assignments.

(vii) difficulties in the nature of course itself.

(viii) lack of contact with the instructor.

(ix) lack of personal interests and,

(x) some other personal problems.

Sloan (1966) made the suggestion for checking the dropout rates, which were should have been extension of period of studies, reduction in number and extent of lessons, thorough response from instructors, more detailed and explanatory lessons etc.

Course Completion

Several factors which could be found to be associated with the completion of courses were highlighted, where as the distance from the place of residence of students to the venue of the institutions, involvement in job and heavy work load were found to be negatively related with course completion.

Studies on Instructional System of Correspondence Education

Discriptive Studies

Studies under this category had aimed at description of students participation in instructional programmes, their study habits, problems in studies etc. A study conducted by Graham (1971) on completion of assignments in Mermods revealed that forty six per cent of students consulted their friends and family members and forty five per cent consulted available literature, and eighteen per cent students left the task unresolved. Forty one per cent students stated that they would have proceeded at the same pace with or without assignments. Twenty one per cent expressed that studies would have been completed slowly without assignments, and thirty seven per cent students that assignments, caused them complete the course more promptly. Very high percentage seventy one per cent of students called for more comprehensive assignments.

Experimentation of Instructional Processes

A few studies were conducted to study the efficiency of certain methods of instruction over other. Willingham's (1971) study aimed at studying comparative effectiveness of combination of different groups of methods viz.,

(i) students meeting the instructors who used lecture cum discussion approaches three times a week.

(ii) students meeting tutors once in a week and taking correspondence study.

(iii) students taking usual correspondence courses.

No significant marks could be in achievement of students who under tool these different methods of instruction. Green (1980), studied the effectiveness of correspondence study methods by using Programmed Learning Material (PLM), Television and home work/assignments. The methods were found to be equally effective in comparision to conventional methods of teaching, as there did not exit significant differences between the achievement scores of students undertaking studies through different methods.

Pfiffer (1971) studied to determine the effect of letters and post cards of encouragement on rate of submission of assignments.

It was found that neither the letters not the post cards of encouragement resulted in a significant increase in the rate of submission of assignments.

Reaction of Students Towards Instructional System

The reaction studies included the responses of students entering the course, dropouts and students completing the courses, opinions about instructional process of correspondence education. Regarding, efficiency of correspondence studies over regular studies, Glatter and Wedell (1971) found that most of the students expressed a high opinion about the correspondence studies provided, they included better quality exercises and test materials., One this matter, Graham (1971) also found that most of the students completing the courses successfully commented similarly. However, they pointed out that better correspondence study depended upon regular study of the texts, self checking exercises followed by assignments and teachers evaluative remarks on them etc. Glatter and Wedell (1971) further found that most of the students of correspondence courses opined that correspondence studies provided more effective exercise and test materials in comparision to part-time oral courses. Also they are more helpful to assess students progress by themselves.

The study of Sloan (1966) pointed out that while reacting to instructional system most of the dropouts stated that correspondence studies required more work and they lessened their interest in the absence of classroom contact.

Problems of Students

The studies like, Powell (1971) and McIntosh (1974) highlighted that several factors like students involvement in job, lack of time and their involvement at home came on the way of academic progress of students.

Suggestions of Students

A few studies (Powell 1971 and Graham 1971) highlighted students' suggestions for improvement of correspondence studies. There students revealed that other than reading texts, additional reference materials such as Television, Cassettes and other communication media be provided; contact with tutors through personal visits, telephone calls etc., be encouraged, more frequent and comprehensive assignments be provided to students.

Comparision of Achievement of Correspondence of Students and Regular Students

In several studies attempts were made to compare the achievement of correspondence education students and regular students taking similar courses. The results sought to be encouraging for correspondence education students. Of course, in some cases they were at par with the results of regular course students. The former kind of results were marked in the case of studies Spencer (1964), as statistically significant differences could be marked between mean average scores of students undertaking correspondence courses and regular courses respectively. The latter kind of results have marked in the study of as no significant differences were marked between the achievement scores of the students of either stream. In no case, however, negative position of correspondence students in comparision with regular students was reported.

Indepth Evaluation Studies

There have been a recent trend in conducting in-depth evaluative studies of instructional system of correspondence education of a particular course/institution. While the evaluative criteria have been varied in nature, there have been efforts to identify different dimensions of instructional programme and to arrive at a holistic picture about this. First, in the case of evaluation of flexi study by Green (1980), its intrinsic worth has been studied in terms of meeting the needs of target group learners, enthusiasm of teachers, appropriate form of correspondence materials and available resources based instruction. Second, applying similar type of references the effectiveness of Emergency Science Programme.

Withe regard to evaluation of instructional programmes at an institution i.e., Distance University in Costa Rica have reported it to be effective as to a large degree it has been achieving its objectives by meeting previously unfulfilled needs at the higher level in the country.

The United Kingdom Open University Student Research Centre has brought a case study, Crooks, Beryl (1987) of the evaluation of one of the United Kingdom Open University

Courses. This evaluation obtained the judgment made by students, staff and external academics.

Cost Analysis

On this area, the findings of a world wide study (Sims, 1978) may be worth its citation. The study revealed that most of the correspondence education processes were established with limited financial backing from educational authorities.

However, the situation changed following better results of the correspondence education systems. With regard to total costs, amount of money spent on current aspects was more than two and a half times that spent on capital costs. The recurring costs stood out as the prominent concern in planning, programming and budgeting for correspondence system of education.

Studies in India

Organisational aspects, pattern, policies and growth. In his exclusive attempt Singh (1977) highlighted the need for correspondence courses in the country, the various stages of preparation and development, the pattern of imparting education through correspondence courses, and the academic and administrative problems being faced by the Institutes. The study also made an assessment of the position and put forward suggestions for future development and streamlining of the system. While analysis of several records, and document enriched the value of the study the experiences of the author have been reflected in the assessment of the position and suggestions for future development.

Further, conducting an empirical study on the trend of enrolment in correspondence courses from 1971 to 1976, Dutt (1976) pointed out that : (1) several correspondence institutions in India were having a very low level of enrolment even after three years of their existence, in some courses even less than 2,000; (2) the overall compound growth rate of enrolment in correspondence education was 8.5 per cent per annum in India during the 5 year period (1971 to 1975). However, the compound growth rate at the post graduate level was 13.1 per cent at PUC/ Intermediate level, it was 11.5 per cent and at the graduate level, it was only 9.7 per cent per annum, (3) While during 1971-1976 the entrance to graduate courses varied from 62 per cent to 66 per cent at post graduate level it increased from 12.8 per cent to 15.8 per cent, (4) the correspondence courses were usually a more extension of the system of regular courses offered through universities.

Biswal's (1979) study which comprised a survey of objectives, staff pattern, enrolment rates, instructional pattern, and finance revealed that :

— the objectives of correspondence institutions imparted through different universities remained similar all over the country;

— most of the courses offered through correspondence system remained similar to those in formal system;

— the academic staff pattern remained more or less similar in all universities whereas differences were marked with regard to administrative staff pattern;

— enrolment rate was found to be higher in Arts, Commerce and education disciplines in comparision to others;

— administrative procedure was found to be liberal in nature. Most of the Directorates of Correspondence Courses (DCCs) did not fix-up a maximum percentage of marks for giving admissions to a course;

— mostly the correspondence materials were presented in essay forms and were despatched to the students without following any rigid system. While in most of the cases compulsion in submission of assignment was insisted, there was no regularity in sending off the evaluated assignments to the students before examination;

— examination pattern of correspondence courses remained similar with that of regular system;

— out of 24 Directorates 7 had regional study centres;

— all the directorates used to conduct PCPs for all courses where lecture method of instruction was given prominence;

— only 12 directorates had library system out of which 3 had postal library system;

— the major sources of finances of the directorates were

students fees, whereas meagre funds were raised through grants from the state Governments and the U.G.C.

Learners of Correspondence System-Characteristics

On these areas a few sample surveys were conducted by Balasubramaniam (1976) on CIEFL, Anand (1979) on under graduate students of Punjab University, Biswal (1979) on M.Ed. Students of the H.P. University and Pillai and Mohan (1983) on the students from all the courses offered by the M.K. University. Regarding the reasons for joining the courses Anand (1979) revealed that 98 per cent of the Pre-University sample students of Punjab University joined the correspondence courses to improve their qualifications and the rest 2 per cent stated for their live for learning. In the same study, while asked about taking up correspondence courses in preference to regular college courses the reasons stated by sample learners were - full time employment (43%), dropping out from the colleges for certain reasons (17%), non availability of admissions in the regular colleges (14%) etc., seventy two per cent of these students hoped to gain better employment by undergoing higher studies and the rest 28 per cent hoped to pursue further studies. Pillai and Mohan (1983) stated more explicitively about the hopes of correspondence students of M.K. University, such as education (39%), Social (18%), Psychological (17%), economic (16%), and occupational (9%). The indicators for these hopes were learners desires for : (1) improving qualifications (26%), (2) learning further (21%), (3) getting financial benefits (11%), improving status (1%), (4) promoting career (6%), (5) utilising leisure (5%), (6) fulfilment of demands (5%), (7) changing the occupations (5%), (8) better job opportunities (4%) etc.

The studies conducted on the background of learners of Punjab University, M.K. University, H.P. University and CIEFL revealed that most of the students belonged to the age group of 20 to 30 (Anand 1979 and Pillai and Mohan 1983), the major chunk of population were men, whereas women constituted a very meagre section i.e., 6 per cent to 7 per cent (Pillai Mohan 1983), in total the SC and ST students' population was less than 10 per cent (Anand 1979 and Pillai and Mohan 1983), the ratio of married students to unmarried once was 1:3 (Anand 1979), 65 per cent students were employed ones (Pillai and Mohan 1983) and belonged to different vocations like teachers (27%), administrative staff (11%), housewives (7%), self-employed (6%), bank employees (3%), business (2%) other educational services (2%), Army (2%) and employed in private undertakings (3%), Studies by (Anand 1979, Biswal 1979 and Pillai and Mohan 1983), found that on an average, the students belonged to lower middle class background.

Balasubramaniam (1976) found that during 1973-75 the dropout rate in CIEFL varied from 57 per cent to 66 per cent. Further, he could identify the non payment of semester fees as major reasons for dropouts. However, there were around 20 per cent to 40 per cent dropouts who could discontinue for reasons other than this.

Instructional Process

Most of the studies conducted so far in India on correspondence education have focussed attention on description of correspondence system of instruction, reaction of students and teachers, comparision of achievements etc. The studies falling on this category were conducted by Bhusan and Sharma (1976) on PCP of H.P. University, Dutt (1976) on 7 different universities of India, Anand (1979) on Punjab University, Panda (1986) on Utkal University, Pandey (1980) on 7 Universities of India, Pillai and Mohan (1983) on M.K.University, Vydehi (1984) on S.V University and Sarwal (1984) on CIEFL.

Regarding study hours of students only Anand (1979) had conducted a small sample survey and reported that on an average a pre university student of Punjab University spent 259 hours per session for completion of studies. In addition to this the student might be taking 70 hours for writing assignments. Further, with regard to study procedures Anand (1979) revealed that 81 per cent of the Pre University students depended upon their instructional processes of correspondence system only and the rest 19 per cent depended upon coaching academy in addition to correspondence system. Forty five per cent students reported to study other notes and digests available in the market in addition to the lesson scripts.

Regarding the usefulness of correspondence lessons it was found by Anand (1979), Biswal (1979 and Pillai and Mohan (1983) that all cases most of the students appreciated them Anand 1979, Biswal 1979 and Pillai and Mohan 1983), while Biswal (1979) found that in the case of H.P. University and Kashmir University assignment system had been found to the useful by most of the students. It was not the case with M.K.University (Pillai and Mohan 1983): Analysing the rate of submission of assignments of Delhi University during 1974-75, Dutt (1976) found that 45.37 per cent students submitted at least 3 assignments per head and nearly 55 per cent students did not submit a singly assignment. As stated by Dutt (1976) and Biswal (1979) all the institutes of correspondence courses had provision of PCPs for all the courses. The PCP attendant analysis done by Anand (1979) revealed that in punjab university from each zone around 40 per cent of pre university students sent their consent to attend the PCP and around 18 per cent students turned up on the first day of registration. However, the attendance gradually decreased over 10 days duration of PCP i.e., only 40 per cent of the registered attendants of 1st days remained present till the 10th day, In all the cases (Anand 1979, Biswal 1979, Pillai and Mohan 1983) most of the students had expressed positive reaction towards the usefulness of PCP. The study had identified such usefulness in the following ways, as stated by most of the students:

— to help in the preparation for examination;

— to cover important and major topics of the syllabus;

— to have deeper understanding over the subject; and

— solving other academic problems.

These areas coincided with the reasons for which the students attended the PCP.

On the opinion of students regarding PCP different studies revealed contradictory facts. Especially, Bhusan and Sharma (1976) found that with regard to compulsion in attendance of PCP most of the M.Ed. students of H.P. University welcomed it. But Anand 1979 reported that the fact was reverse in the case of Punjab University. Study by Anand (1979) revealed that most of the Punjab University students opined for organisation of PCP twice in a session with 7 days duration each. Bhushan and Sharma (1976) in H.P. University most of the M.Ed. Students opined for 15 days duration of PCP in each semester was needed. Other common results as reflected by the above studies on PCP were that most of the students preferred coverage of all the topics in gist during the

PCP while giving prior importance to difficult topics; lectures should be followed by discussion; correspondence institute should arrange boarding and lodging for the students; library facility be made available to students during PCP, experts of repute in various areas should be invited to deliver lectures in PCP etc.

Studies of Pillai and Mohan 1983) showed that most of the students who had competed correspondence courses from M.K. University found different aspects of correspondence instruction viz., lesson scripts, assignments, PCPs, regional study centres and radio broadcasts programmes useful.

The study of Biswal (1979) focusing on the problems faced by the heads of the institutions and departments, teachers and students revealed that:

— identification of experts to write the lessons, selection of appropriate number of teachers for evaluation of assignments, delay in receiving the assignments from students and evaluation of assignments, lack of co-ordination between directorates and regular teaching departments of the university were the problems for most of the heads of the institutions and departments of all directorates;

— insufficient time provided for writing lessons, excess number of assignments given for correction and limited time provided for completing specified courses during PCP were the problems for most of the teachers of all the directorates;

— supply of inadequate length of correspondence materials, lesser time provided for writing assignments, inadequate guidelines given for writing assignments, non-availability of sufficient reference books were the subject of complaint of most of the M.Ed. students of H.P. University.

Vydehi (1984) evaluated the presentation of 1st year degree general English course of S.V. University with regard to satisfaction of students' needs, attainment of objectives of course and nature of the instructional processes and evaluation procedures adopted. Analysis of aims of English teaching methods of instruction, reaction of students and teachers and observation of PCP, were done to locate the weaknesses of the present structure of curriculum. The author prepared an alternative 'student active instructional format' and a new type of distance teaching material. The achievement comparision of students undertaking conventional approach and modified approach revealed results in favour of the modified approach. A similar kind of study has been undertaken by Sarwal (1984) for preparation of teacher training correspondence course units for English language teaching in CIEFL.

The achievement studies reflected divergent facts regarding the strength of correspondence instruction in comparision to regular course instruction in India. Panda (1980) found no significant difference between the achievement of under graduate students of correspondence and regular streams of Delhi University and Utkal University respectively. However, in the cases of rest of the studies mixed results were identified. Anand (1979) found that in the Punjab University the pass percentage of correspondence students were lower than of overall university level with regard to pre-university and B.A. I Courses, whereas the facts were reverse with regard to B.A. II and B.A. III courses. The second class holders percentages were higher in the cases of pre-university, B.A. - I and B.A. - III courses of correspondence streams. Biswal (1979) found that there was no significant difference between academic achievement of correspondence and regular stream students with regard to M.A. English an B.A. courses of Punjabi University. However, the regular stream students of M.A. Punjabi course and B.A. course of Punjabi University and M.K. University respectively had scored higher than the correspondence steam students of similar courses. Pandey 1980) found that at over all courses levels in Meerut, Delhi, Punjab, Punjabi, Mumbai, Sri Venateswara and Madurai Kamaraj Universities, the pass percentages of correspondence streams were higher than those of regular streams. Further, it was found that the proportion of third division holders was higher in correspondence stream than that regular stream. Comparatively the regular stream produced more graduates with first and second divisions.

Rathore (1991) studied on the treatment given to assignment responses at the correspondence institutes. He developed the questionnaire on 'Students Feedback' for the project work submitted to National Institute of Educational Planning and Administration (NIEPA), New Delhi. The questionnaire was designed on the basis of the 'Total Design Method'. He found that 30.51 per cent of the students received only checked assignments, and 254.32 per cent of them in addition also got marks. Thus, in the case of exactly 55.83 per cent of the students neither comments nor model solutions were given in response to the assignments submitted by them. Only 8.44 per cent of the students got model solution/answers in response to their assignments. Besides, general checking, tutors wrote comments in the case of 16.88 per cent of the students ; and in the case of 28.83 per cent, they also gave personel suggestions to correct mistakes and suggest materials for further reading. Putting the last two together the finding is that comments of one or the other type were given on assignment responses only in the case of 35.71 per cent of the students.

Zacharia et al. (1983) conducted studies on the application of distance model of learning for regular on campus students in the teaching of pharmacology at Christian Medical College, Ludhiana and gave detailed result of his study as follows:

(a) Passive role imposed on the students.

(b) No learner-autonomy in terms of time and content.

(c) No provision for providing feedback to the students except during the term-end examinations.

(d) No indication to the students regarding the subject matter to be covered.

(e) Evaluation based mainly on recall, giving little opportunity to the students to use their cognitive skills.

Sesharatnam (1994) conducted study on Multi Media package in the Open University system. The study revealed.

(a) There is some difference between the course material of open university and conventional universities.

(b) Academic counsellors and students felt that course material were only partly self instructional.

(c) Television broadcasts, though an important components of Distance Learning System is not yet used by the university.

(d) For effective use of the provision of audio, video programmes to students, study centres lack necessary physical infrastructure and trained man power.

An Overview

The above presentation gives a hint about the research efforts on certain major aspects of Distance Education at university stage. The major focus of researches at this stage had been mostly exploration of facts on different aspects of the system viz., organisation pattern and growth, assessment of needs of learners, learners' needs for joining the courses, and characteristics of learners and dropouts; different aspects of instructional system; and achievement of learners.

There is little doubt about the contribution of these studies in supplying first hand information about the nature and status of Distance education in deferent countries. The facts arrived at also tell about the functioning pattern of such systems to some extent. However, most of these studies have been conducted in isolated form. They, too, have chosen different variables for investigation in unrelated form. As a result the complexities involved in the organisation and functioning of the instructional system have not been brought to the focus. Whether, at institutional level or at national level, very few efforts have been made to develop comprehensive view about the functioning of the system.

There have been studies aiming at evaluation of the system. While, most of them have considered achievement as the major criterion of evaluation, in some cases the opinions of participants of the system have been considered as other parameters of evaluation.

The studies conducted so far, in India are either generalising or institutional type, exploring certain base line data about the system in piecemeal form. Mostly, they have provided hints for undertaking further investigations on certain broad issues cutting across the institutional variations.

Also they have generated scope for looking at certain context oriented problems at institutional level. However, in spite of the availability of these generalised studies, little attempt has been made to analyse and consolidate the facts as explored by all the studies on different aspects of the system at national level.

Most of the investigations are at Micro level, Piecemeal, informative and did not take into account the context of the overall functioning of the system. The investigational have also not focussed on the qualitative aspects of the performance of the students of the two systems viz., Distance Education and conventional. Some of them emphasised the holistic model of investigation, looking at the intricate relationship of influential factors in single institutional programmes. In points out the need for making attempts at studying the Distance Education System of a region as a whole. There is also a need for evaluating the effectiveness of Distance Education System in Indian context.

Method of Investigation

Introduction

The review of related literature presented in previous chapter enabled the choosing of the method of investigation for this study and, in the construction of the tools for gathering data.

Distance Education as a system caters to the needs of the clientele group, fulfilling the specific objectives of access, relevance and, motivation. The investigation was taken up with the premise that the role of Distance Education in catering to the goals of higher education is unquestionable. The only question that educationists have to answer is, how best to improve the Distance Education machinery to cater to the changing goals of higher education.

The review of related literature also pointed out, that not much of research work is done in the area of effectiveness of Distance Education system for realising the changing goals of higher education. Distance Education caters to the concept of continuing education and to the educational needs of population. The scope of educational process in a society is enlarged through Distance Education System. Its importance and contribution to the modern progressive societies is universally accepted.

As already pointed out, the main focus of this piece of research work was to find out whether Distance Education System in Andhra Pradesh is effective to realise goals of higher education. One aim was to analyse the Distance Education System in two typical contexts, in terms of selected institutional growth parameters over the years. Another aim was to interview the faculty and the learners in the Distance Education System for eliciting their opinions about the main features of this system. It was felt that, a combination of trend analysis data and opinions will yield the necessary information to answer the research question of the study.

Selection of Institutions for the Study

The School of Distance Education (SDE) of Andhra University, affiliated to a conventional University an BRAOU which was started by Government of Andhra Pradesh, in line with policy on Distance Education in India are the two oldest Distance Education institutions of the state. They represent the Distance Education System in Andhra Pradesh. Hence, these two institutions were selected.

The following are the profiles of the two institutions:

School of Distance Education, Andhra University A Brief Profile

1. The School of Correspondence Course was established in the year 1972 with an enrolment of 355 students. It has crossed an enrolment of 45,000 during the academic year 1996-97.

2 (a). The Staff pattern consists of One Director, Eleven Deputy Directors, Seventeen Assistant Directors, Nine administrative staff and one Librarian. The Directors and Assistant Directors are specialists in their own disciplines and perform, the main functions of co-ordination, extention, and teaching.

(b) The Flow Chart of Administration of School of Distance Education follows:

(c) The school was headed by Honorary Directors from its inception until 1982, when a full-time Director was appointed by the University authorities.

3. At present, in all, the school of Distance Education is offering nineteen courses in various disciplines.

4 (a). The method of 'Open University System' has been implemented by this school from 1976.

(b) The school introduced liberalised admissions into B.A. and B.Com. Degree Courses. But, the candidate should complete 18 Years of age by 1st July of the year of

Flow Chart of Administration

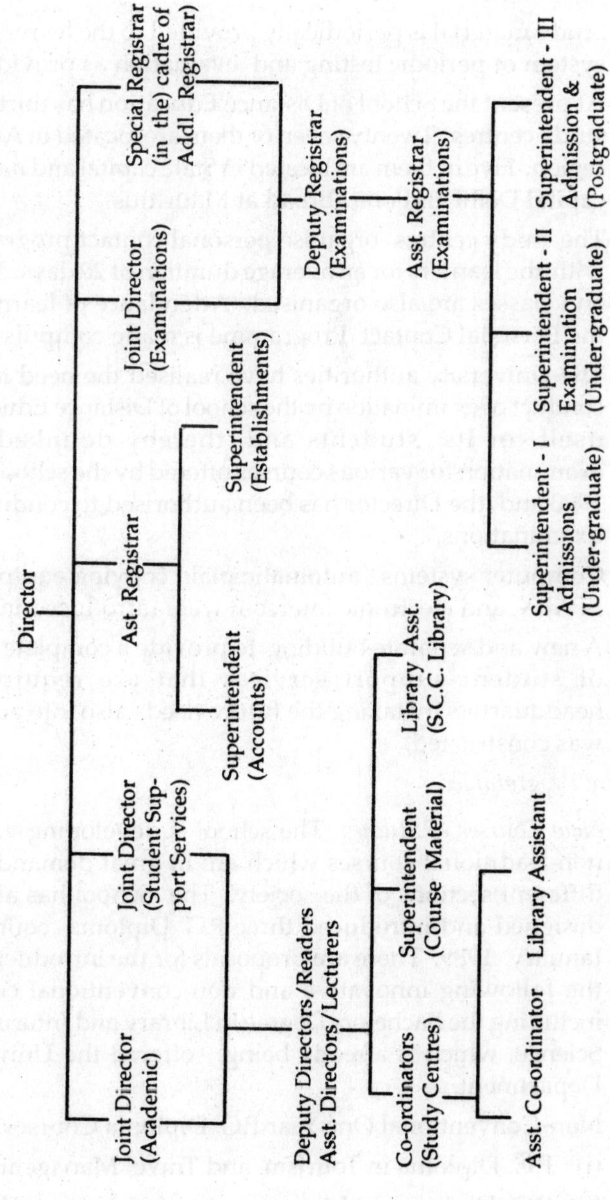

appearance to the Entrance Examination.

5. Study material is periodically provided to the learner and, system of periodic testing and evaluation is provided.
6. At present the School of Distance Education has thirty two study centres. Twenty seven of them are located in Andhra region. Five of them are located in State capital and national capital Delhi and one abroad at Mauritius.
7. The study centres organise personal contact programme with the learners for an average duration of 20 days. Week-end classes are also organised. Attendance of learners at the Personal Contact Programme is made compulsory.
8. The University authorities have realised the need for the conduct of examination by the school of Distance Education itself for its students and, thereby delinked the examination for various courses offered by the school from 1990 and, the Director has been authorised to conduct the Examinations.
9. Computer systems, automatic plain copying equipment, EPABX, and electronic intercom were introduced in 1990.
10. A new and separate building to provide a complete range of student support services that are required at headquarters by taking the future needs also into account was constructed.

11. *Future Programmes*

(A) *New Courses of Study* : The school is developing various non-traditional courses which are in great demand from different sections of the society. The School has already designed and introduced three P.G. Diploma courses in January, 1989. There are proposals for the introduction of the following innovative and non-conventional courses including the Bachelors Degree in Library and Information Science, which is already being offered the University Department.

(a) Non-Conventional One Year P.G. Diploma Courses:

(i) P.G. Diploma in Tourism and Travel Management.

(ii) P.G. Diploma in Management of Voluntary Welfare Organisations.

(iii) P.G. Diploma on Personnel Management, Industrial Relations and Labour Welfare.

(iv) P.G. Diploma in Computer Programming and Applications.

(b) One-year Course already offered by the University Department:

(v) Bachelor Degree in Library and Information Science.

(c) One-Year Diploma Courses.

(vi) Diploma in Village Administration Development.

(d) Awareness Course with no minimum qualification and, examination for people with minimum age of 20 years.

(vii) Telugu Culture and Heritage (A Certificate of completion of course will be issued without any examination).

(B) *Research in Distance Education*

There are proposals to involve teachers of the school in pursuing research work in the area of Distance Education, both at the theoretical level as a discipline and, at the practical level to evaluate organisational aspects of the system; without prejudice to the research work in their respective subjects of specialisation of the conventional pattern, and in undertaking guidance to students for M.Phil and Ph.D. Degrees in various aspects of Distance Education.

(C) *Creation of Information and Publicity Cell*

The students of school of Distance Education, A.U., are spread throughout the country and abroad particularly in Mauritius and it is highly desirable to disseminate information pertaining to the various programmes, courses of the school and also to provide guidance to the learners on variety of administrative as well as academic needs. At present the school provides information/ guidance through circulars, news items etc., and its study centres are also being used to supply the information.

In order to strengthen its publicity campaign, and to attract a larger number of women and backward sections of society, the school proposes to create full-fledged information and publicity cells at its headquarters and some of its study centres where its student population are concentrated and where there is much potential to attract a sizeable number of prospective learners to its courses. These proposed cells with make necessary arrangements to provide publicity material, brochures, prospectus, admission forms etc. To make the effective functioning of the cells, it was proposed to have mobile publicity vans and computer systems.

(D) *Organising Workshops and Training Programmes*

In order to transform the present course material into self-instructional Distance Education format, workshops as well as training programmes are to be organised on a regular basis for the resources persons including the teaching staff of Distance Education Institutions. In this connection, the School has already conducted two orientation programmes for the conversion of existing study material into self-instructional format. More such programmes are proposed to be conducted in order to train the teachers at both graduate and post-graduate level.

(E) *Strenthening of Students Support Services*

Establishment of study centres at the needy places and manning these centres on a full-fledged basis with all the necessary support services including library facilities, personal contact programmes, weekend classes, play back of Audio and Video Cassettes, radio broadcasts and T.V. telecasts etc., strengthen correspondence institutions. The reports acknowledge that, there is a need to strengthen the existing study centres besides, starting new study centres depending upon the need and potential for development. In order to provide the package of the recommended services at the study centers, there are proposals to have a full-fledged library and an information cell supported with computerised systems, Audio Visual equipment etc.

(F) *Building*

At present the school of Distance Education is situated in a three storied building and a need is felt to have at lest two additional floors to strengthen its physical facilities.

Profiles of Dr. B.R. Ambedkar Open University

(i) Dr., B.R. Ambedkar Open University was set up in August, 1982 by an Act of Andhra Pradesh Legislature. The establishment of BRAOU was a great landmark in the history of Distance

Education in India. It heralded a new era in India's higher education.

Special Features

The significant features of BRAOU are:

— State-wide Jurisdiction.

— Flexible admission rules.

The age for entrance eligibility is 20 years and there are formal and non formal entrance into the Distance Education System.

— Individualised study.

— Flexibility in terms of place, pace and tone of study.

— Use of modern information and, communication technologies.

— Student support services for academic and, administrative help.

— Comprehensive evaluation system.

Organisational Structure

(i) The Governor of Andhra Pradesh is the Chancellor of the University.

(ii) The Board of Management, Academic Senate, Planning and Monitoring Board and Finance Committee are the important authorities of the University.

(iii) The Vice-Chancellor, Rector, Directors, Deans, Registrar, Finance Officer are the main offices of the University Division and faculties are the main components of the University.

(iv) In all these matters, the provision of the Act of the BRAOU are similar to those other Acts in the state.

The following is organisation structure of this University.

Instructional System

Course Material

(a) The University adopts a multi-media approach for instruction, printed course material, radio lessons, audio and Video lessons, contact-cum counselling classes, winter and summer schools for intensive coaching by experts on important topics.

Organisational Structure of the University

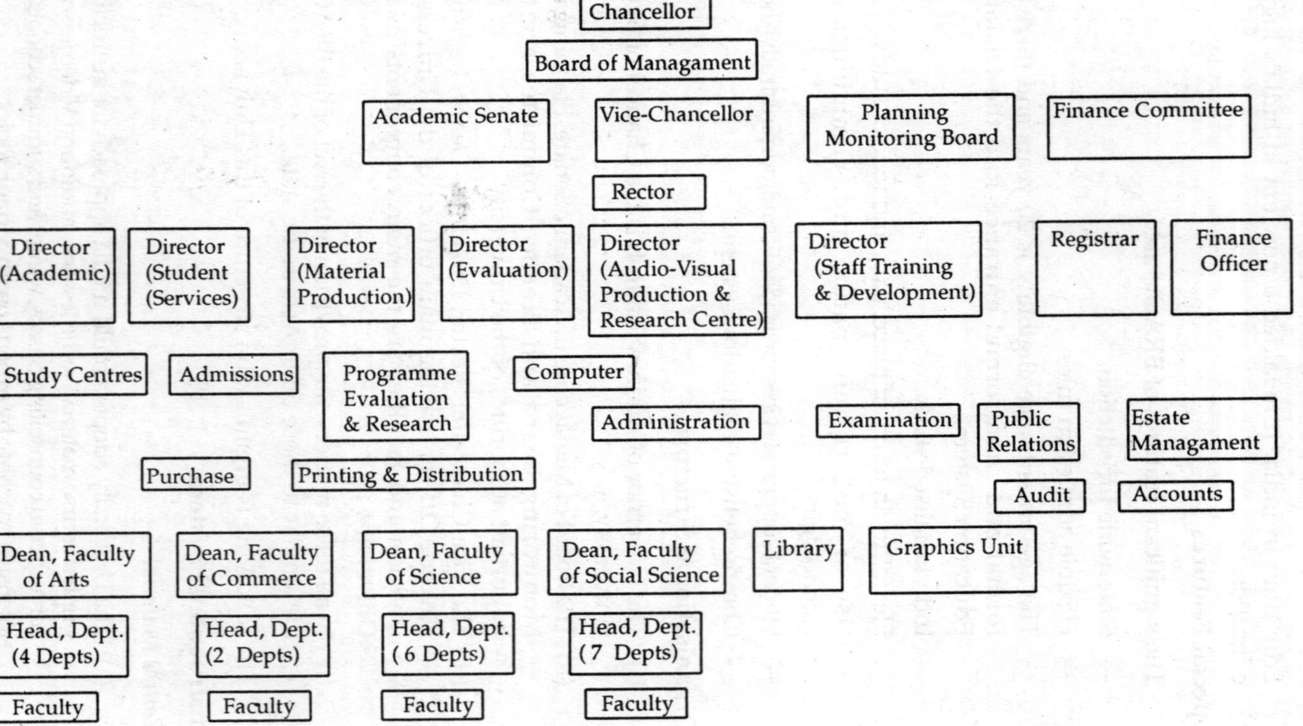
Chancellor
Board of Managament
Academic Senate
Vice-Chancellor
Planning Monitoring Board
Finance Committee
Rector
Director (Academic)
Director (Student (Services)
Director (Material Production)
Director (Evaluation)
Director (Audio-Visual Production & Research Centre)
Director (Staff Training & Development)
Registrar
Finance Officer
Study Centres
Admissions
Programme Evaluation & Research
Computer
Administration
Examination
Public Relations
Estate Managament
Purchase
Printing & Distribution
Audit
Accounts
Dean, Faculty of Arts
Dean, Faculty of Commerce
Dean, Faculty of Science
Dean, Faculty of Social Science
Library
Graphics Unit
Head, Dept. (4 Depts)
Head, Dept. (2 Depts)
Head, Dept. (6 Depts)
Head, Dept. (7 Depts)
Faculty
Faculty
Faculty
Faculty

(b) The course material in each subject is prepared by a team of course editors, course writers and translators.

(c) The course teams also identify the topics for the preparation of radio, audio and video lessons which are produced in collaboration with the university's Audio Visual production and Research Centres.

(d) The University has so far published 250 volumes of course materials covering as many as thirty different disciplines.

Student Support Services (SSS)

The Student Support Services (SSS) are to help students to overcome barriers to learning, which result from the loneliness of the student working on his own.

(i) The students are supported in variety of ways by Distance Education Institution.

(ii) To enable the students to have regular contact with the University, study centers have been established, 107 in number throughout the state. Besides, there are 12 Post Graduate study centres.

(iii) Delhi, Madras and Bangalore include Post Graduate Study centres. These centres provide opportunities for student-teacher and student-student interaction.

(iv) The study centers provides general information, admission-related guidance and counselling.

(v) The study centers are located in the existing educational institutions and, normally function on all holidays and Sundays and in the evenings on working days.

(vi) Each study center is provided with a V.C.R. and a T.V. set for Video lessons. It is also supplied, with audio cassettes in sufficient number for the students to listen to audio lessons.

(vii) The study centre also makes available to its students copies of the radio time-tables indicating the titles of the lessons broadcast by the A.I.R., Hyderabad on its B Transmission. The radio lessons are broadcasted five days a week.

(viii) The Mobile science laboratory van will provide laboratory training to science students of the University even in the remote areas of the state with the slogan of the university "Education at your Doorstep".

Audio Visual Production and Research Centre

The Audio Visual Production and Research Centre (AVP and RC) of the University was started in 1985. Since 1983 the university has been broadcasting its syllabus oriented educational lessons of the courses offered, over All India Radio in English, Telugu, Hindi and Urdu.

To augment the production of audio video packages as part of course material, the AVP and RC has been upgraded to fulfledged Directorate in 1993. Major functions of the centre are to :

(a) Produce Audio and Video programmes.

(b) Organise Education Television/Radio broadcasts and

(c) Undertake Research in the field of audio visual production and utilisation as applied to Distance Education.

Research

The University had developed collaboration with the Centre for Economics and Social Studies for M.Phil. and Ph.D. Programmes. It will admit students in two streams formal and non formal. While formal stream will comprise students with the usual eligibility requirements, the non-formal stream will be based on the candidate's outstanding contribution to his field without having any formal university based qualifications. This would be in tune with the concept of the open university system in which flexibility and wider access to higher education are stressed.

As per the BRAOU, Hand Book, 1993-94, Twenty two M.Phil. Degrees were awarded. There was no mention of Ph.D., degrees.

Evaluation

In BRAOU, there is a separate Directorate of Distance Education Research in Centre for evaluation (CFE).

Objectives of Centre for Evaluation

(i) to plan and carry out both extensive and intensive research on various aspects of Distance Education,

(ii) to evolve research based alternatives for improving the instructional process at various level,

(iii) to strengthen teaching in academic programmes at undergraduate and post-graduate levels,

(iv) to strengthen research at M.Phil. and Ph.D. levels,

(v) to provide for dissemination of research finding in the field of Distance Education, and

(vi) to act as a critical friend in the process of formative evaluation of courses.

Future Programmes

According to BRAOU Vice-Chancellor's interview with "Eenadu" Daily on 27-04-1997.

Besides the 107 study centres and 12 post-graduate study centres, it is proposed to open seven more regional study centres in the state and study centres in gulf countries. There is a proposal to start new courses viz.,B.A. Office Management, Environmental Studies, B.Sc., Nursing, Diploma in Ground Water Management, Diploma in Women Studies, Diploma in Environmental Planning, Pharmacy and Post Graduate Courses in Sciences.

METHOD AND DESIGN OF THE STUDY

As reported in the previous pages, Distance Education Institutions in Andhra Pradesh were chosen to gather data for answering the research question. The profiles of two institutions were described. It was felt that, the date from the concerned institutions, along with opinions gathered through interview and opinionnaire respectively from the faculty and learners will be representative of the Distance Education System in the State.

This study comes under descriptive research and adopts a combination of trend analysis and survey approach. The major objective of this study was to evaluate the effectiveness of the Distance Education System in realising the goals of higher education in Andhra Pradesh. It was proposed to answer the research question by :

(a) Identifying the evaluating the growth trends in Distance Education System in Andhra Pradesh.

(b) Identifying the areas in this system that need to be strengthened and, evaluating its effectiveness in goal realisation with the help of the above data.

Conclusions are drawn by studying the selected representative institutions of the Distance Education System in Andhra Pradesh. The details of methods and tools for gathering data and procedures

Table 3.5

Design of the Study

Topic : Effectiveness of Distance Education System in Andhra Pradesh for Realising Goals of Higher Education.

Research Method Chosen : Descriptive Method — Trend Analysis and Survey

Institutions : 1. School of Distance Education, Andhra University, Vishakhapatnam
2. BRAOU, Hyderabad

Sl.No. Purpose	*Sources of Data*	*Instruments Used*	*Sample and Selection Procedure*	*Data Collection Procedures*	*Analysis of Data*
1. Opinions about Goal Realisation Through Distance Education System in Andhra Pradesh.	(a) Faculty	Interview schedule	30 Purposive Sampling	Interview	Descriptive and Summarisation
	(a) Learners	Opinionnaire 3 point scale	400 Quota Sampling	Administration of Opinionnaire	Frequency counting percentages
2. Identifying areas of Distance Education System that need strengthening	(a) Faculty	Interview schedule	30 Purposive Sampling	Interview	Descriptive and Summarisation
	(a) Learners	Opinionnaire 3 point scale	400 Quota Sampling	Administration of Opinionnaire	Frequency Counting Percentages
3. Growth Trends	Officials records Annual reports Evaluation reports	Preparing Statistical table from available sources	Office records of BRAOU and SDE	Observation	Descriptive analysis of growth trends

followed in analysis of data for this study follow.

Table 3.5 gives the design of the study.

Constrction of Tools

I. *Interview Schedule for Faculty Members*

An open ended interview schedule was prepared.

The interview schedule for the faculty members was prepared, mainly keeping in view the areas of higher education that need to be strengthened.

- National Policy on Educational 1986, has emphasised that there is a need for consolidation and expansion of facilities in the existing institutions of higher education with a view of maintenance of quality and standards and, students strength.
- It has also recommended the development of autonomous colleges with their own system of evaluation.
- It has highlighted the need for re-designing of courses: to meet the growing demands of specialisation, to provide flexibility in the combination of courses, to facilitate mobility among courses, programmes and institutions, to update and modernise curricula, to integrate work-practice experience and participation in creative activities with the learning process, and to facilitate reforms in the evaluation procedure.
- The need for training teachers in the higher education system was stressed. Recommendations for in service education of teachers in higher education were made.
- Research in Universities was another aspect, emphasising the need for research facilities in higher education.
- The need for improving efficiency in higher education institutions through modern administrative procedures, library councils for higher education for co-ordination and National apex body was pointed out. It was envisaged that the establishment of National apex body will bring about greater co-ordination and integration in planning and development of higher education system, including research.

— Finally, it recommended that measures are to be undertaken in higher education to facilitate inter-regional mobility by providing equal access to every Indian of requisite merit regardless of his origin.

A copy of the interview schedule administered on the faculty of the two Distance Education Institutions of the study is given below.

Interview Schedule

1. Do you think that the Distance Education System in the state is helping in realisation of the goals of higher education? Why? How?
2. Do you think that there is a need for expansion of Distance Education Institutions in the State?
3. Do you feel that the academic faculties in Distance Education System have enough autonomy? Why?
4. Do you think that there is a need for re-designing courses in Distance Education System?
5. Do you think that the Distance Education is playing a role in producing and training teachers for the educational system?
6. What are your suggestions for strengthening research in the Distance Education System?
7. What are the areas of Distance Education System that need to be strengthened?
   (a) Improvement of Facilities.
   (b) Study Centres.
   (c) Personal Contact Programmes.
   (d) Usage of multi-media.
   (e) Study of materials for learners.
8. Do you think that there is a need for national apex body to monitor the Distance Education System in our country/state?
9. Do you think that in Distance Education System the learner has mobility?

   Ex: (a) Freedom to choose courses,
   (b) Rules and regulations,
   (c) Freedom to move from one institution to another institution.

II. *Construction of Opinionnaire for the Learners*

After reviewing the related literature, and discussions with colleagues and experts in the field of higher education, an opinionnaire was prepared to ascertain the opinions of learners on the effectiveness of Distance Education in realising the goals of higher education.

Opinions were gathered from the students of Distance Education System by asking them to evaluate the Distance Education System with reference to the following aspects.

(a) Overall facilities in the system.

(b) Courses, curriculum and evaluation.

(c) Student support services like :

- (i) Assignments, Course material, Study Centres,
- (ii) Personal Contact Programme,
- (iii) Counselling,
- (iv) Multi-media.

(d) Difficulties faced by the students in the system

(e) Students were also asked to give their opinions about the goals of H.E. that are being realised by the Distance Education System.

Validity

The preliminary draft was submitted to a panel of judges for identifying statement relevance, suitability for answering the research question and, repetitiveness. The final items selected by the judges are considered to be having content validity and conceptual validity. Since the tool is not an attitude scale, the investigator did not undertake statistical validation of the tool.

Areawise Opinion statements of this tool follow:

OPINIONNAIRE FOR STUDENTS

Area I : Overall facilities in Distance Education System.

1. Distance Education Universities/Directorates are accessible to students in seeking information.
2. The admission procedures are systematic.

3. The facilities at study centres are very useful to students.
4. The infrastructure facilities (Building, Classrooms, Library, P.C.P. Centres etc.), offer adequate accommodation.

Area II : Curriculum, courses and, evaluation.

1. There is a need to introduce more courses.
2. There is a need of continuous evaluation in courses.
3. Evaluation procedures should be improved.
4. Courses are suitable to the needs of the students.
5. More job oriented courses should be introduced.
6. The Distance Education Curriculum is very relevant to student needs.
7. There is a need for introducing teacher education courses like B.Ed.

Area III : Student Support Services.
(Courses material, Assignments, study centres, P.C.Ps, multi-media)

1. Course material is supplies in time.
2. Course material is covering the entire syllabus.
3. Assignment approach is properly followed.
4. Assignment is given in terms of instructional goals.
5. Study centres are quite useful.
6. Counselling timings are suitable to students.
7. The quality of counselling in satisfactory.
8. Personal contact programmes (P.C.P.) are beneficial to students.
9. The teacher-student rapport during P.C.P. is encouraging.
10. P.C.P. dates are convenient to students.
11 Multi-media (Radio broadcast, audio cassettes, video cassettes and T.V.) are used effectively.

Area IV : Realisation of the goals of Higher Education

They were also asked to give their opinions about the goals of higher education that are being realised by the Distance Education System with the help of the following statements.

1. Distance Education approach helps in understanding social issues in the country.
2. Distance Education gives opportunity to understand economic issues in the country.
3. Enables me to understand moral and spiritual issues faced by mankind.
4. Allows me to understand Indian culture.
5. Gives scope to know cultural issues in the world.
6. Distance Education promotes the acquisition of specialised knowledge.
7. Develops specialised skills.
8. Helps to contribute to National Development.
9. Distance Education guides the students to opt for teaching profession.

Area V : Aspects relating to difficulties faced by the students.

1. Admission procedures
2. Payment of fees.
3. Eligibility Certification.
4. Learning material.
5. Information about P.C.P.
6. Attending P.C.P.
7. Library Services.
8. Counselling by counsellors.
9. Examination dates.
10. Publication of examination results.

Reliability

The tool for the learners of Distance Education was not administered on a try out sample. The tool consists of a total number of 41 statements to which the sample responded on a three point scale, of Agreement, Undecided, Disagreement with the statement. For calculating the reliability, the tool was divided into two halves. An individual's score on the first twenty one statements was the first half and the score on the second last 20 items was second half. For each individual, the split-half scores were calculated for the total sample of 400 respondents.

By using the split-half method the reliability coefficient of the tool was found. The reliability coefficient of the tool administered on Distance Education learners was 0.809.

TREND ANALYSIS

Best (1986) says that: The trend Study is an interesting application of the descriptive method. In essence it is based upon a longitudinal consideration of recorded data, indicating what has been happening in the past, what the present situation reveals, and on the basis of these data, what is likely to happen in the future.

Lokesh Koul says (1984) that, trend studies are undertaken through documentary analysis or survey at repeated intervals.

The purpose of trend analysis in this study is to analyse documentary data from two types of distance education institutions namely BRAOU and School of Distance Education of Andhra University, in terms of selected institutional growth parameters. The parameters chosen were:

1. Student enrolment.
2. Income and expenditure growth.
3. Successful courses completion by students.
4. Growth in number of disciplines.
5. Growth in research.
6. Growth in study centres.
7. Growth in use of multi-media.

Sources of Data for Trend Analysis

To gather data for trend analysis, the investigator visited the administrative offices of BRAOU and school of Distance Education of Andhra University, Vishakhapatnam. The investigator could gather the following document which were used to develop the trend tables. The documents from School of Distance Education, Andhra University, Vishakhapatnam.

1. A Status Report — School of Distance Education, 1997.
2. Profile, School of Distance Education.

3. Budget Reports — 1987-88 to 1996-97.
4. Annual Reports — 1988-1995.

The documents from BRAOU are :

1. Hand Book — 1993-94.
2. A Profile — Audio Video Production and Research Centre, 1995.
3. Students enrolment pattern in undergraduate programme (A Study) 1995.
4. Funding of Distance Education: A case study of an Open University — 1994.
5. Budge Reports. 1983-84 to 1992-93, 1994 to 97, 1993-94 not available.
6. Distance Education, Research in Centre for Evaluation — A Review.

Sampling, Administration and Scoring of Tools

(a) *Interview Schedule*

As already reported, an open ended interview schedule for Faculty members of Distance Education System was prepared. The sample for the interviews was selected from the faculty working in the academic head quarters of the two Distance Education Institution. The faculty related to study centres was not included for conducting the interviews. The interviews were conducted on the basis of availability of the faculty members. Fifteen faculty members from BRAOU, Hyderabad and fifteen from School of Distance Education, Visakhapatnam were contacted.

It was felt that this sample of faculty at the helm of affairs in the Open University and School of Distance Education is a purposive sample, because they belong to the group of individuals involved in the process of planning, administering and evaluating the process of Distance Education. The interview data was recorded, consolidated and verbally analysed. No statistical treatment was given to the interview schedule data. The description of the interview sample in terms of their designations, educational qualifications and nature of job is shown in the coming pages.

Table 3.6

Discription of Interview Sample

SDE	*Designation*	*Educational Qualification*	*Nature of the Job*
1.	Director	M.A., Ph.D., D.A.S.	Director of the S.D.E.
Deputy Director (D.D.)/Reader			
2.	D.D.	M.A., Ph.D.	Administration
3.	Reader	M.A., M.A.,Ph.D.,M.Ed.	Teaching
4.	D.D.	M.Com., Ph.D.	Financial Officer
5.	D.D.	M.A.,M.A.A,Ph.D.	Computer Section Incharge
6.	Reader	M.Com., Ph.D.	Teaching
7.	D.D.	M.A., Ph.D.	Production in-charge
8.	Reader	M.A., Ph.D.	Teaching
Assistant Director (A.D.)/Lecturer			
9.	A.D.	M.A., Ph.D.	Admn./Teaching
10.	A.D.	M.A., Ph.D.	Teaching
11.	A.D.	M.A., Ph.D.	Admn./Teaching
12.	A.D.	M.A., Ph.D.	Teaching
13.	A.D.	M.A., M.A., DSS, Ph.D.	Teaching/Admn.
14.	A.D.	M.A., M.Ed., M.Phil, Ph.D.	Admn./Teaching
15.	A.D.	M.A.	Teaching

Table 3.7

Discription of Interview — Sample Open University

BRAOU	*Deisgnation*	*Educational Qualifications*	*Nature of Job*
1.	Prof.	M.A., Ph.D.	Teaching
2.	Associate Prof.	M.A., Ph.D.	Teaching
3.	Associate Prof.	M.A., Ph.D.	Teaching
4.	Associate Prof.	M.Sc., Ph.D.	Teaching
5.	Associate Prof.	M.A., Ph.D.	Teaching
6.	Associate Prof.	M.Sc., Ph.D.	Teaching
7.	Prof.	M.Sc., Ph.D.	Director, A.V. Production
8.	Deputy Director	M.A.	A.V. Production & Research Centre — Producer
9.	Associate Prof.	M.Sc., M.Ed., Ph.D.	Director I/C, Centre for evalation
10.	Deputy Director	M.A., Ph.D.	Administration/Coordination

(Contd.)

BRAOU	*Deisgnation*	*Educational Qualifications*	*Nature of Job*
11.	Deputy Director	M.Com., Ph.D.	Director I/C, Dept. of Publications
12.	Deputy Director	M.A., Ph.D.	Administration/Coordination
13.	Asst. Director	M.Com., Ph.D.	Administration/Dept. of Publications
14.	A.D.	M.A., Ph.D.	Administration/Coordination
15.	A.D.	M.A., Ph.D.	Administration/Coordination

(a) *Opinionnaire for Learners :*

Sampling Procedures : The population of Distance Learners in the above two institutions is widely distributed geographically throughout Andhra Pradesh. The total picture of Distançe Education Learners in the two institutes could not be secured from office records. Hence it was opined that securing a proper representative sample of learners of Distance Education System is possible by applying the principle of Quota sampling to the available information:

> Garret says that (1985): stratified or quota sampling also çalled "Controlled" sampling is a technique designed to ensure representativeness and avoid bias by use of a modified random sampling method. This scheme is applicable when the population is composed of subgroups or strata of different sizes, so that a representative sample must contain individuals drawn from each category or stratum in accordance with the sizes of the sub groups with in each stratum or subgroup the sampling is random or as nearly so as possible.

The coursewise enrolment figures for the two Distance Education Institutions for the year 1995-96, could be secured.

The following Tables show the total students on rolls in SDE and OU for the year 1995-96 and the sample chosen.

Administration of Student Opinionnaire

The only time for contacting these students was during Personal Contact Programme (PCP). The PCP centres were accessible and it was possible to administer the tool on the students in an as is where is basis. After gathering the list of study centres, the study centres where the tool is to be administered were randomly selected.

Table 3.8

Sample Description — Quota Sample Allotment on the Basis of Enrolment of Students — 1995-96 — SDE

School of Distance Education	*B.A.*	*B.Com.*	*M.Com.*	*B.Ed.*	*M.Ed.*	*Introductory Courses*	*B.Sc.*	*P.G.Dcrs*	*PGIIP*	*M.A. Courses*	*Total*
Student on rolls during 1995-96	33,300	6,500	600	350	100	302	577	115	205	2,555	46,639
Size of Quota Sample	143	29	3	2	2	2	3	2	2	12	200

Table 3.9

Sample Description — Quota Sample Allotment of the Basis of Enrolment of Students — 1995-96 — BRAOU

BRAOU	*U. G. Degree*	*Dip. in Pub. Acc.*	*BPR*	*BLI. SC.*	*DPFN*	*P.G. Degree MBA/M.Sc./M.A.*	*Total*
Student on rolls during 1995-96	40,000	--	250	325	--	1130	41,705
Size of Quota Sample	190	--	2	2	--	6	200

The Opinionnaire was administered on a total sample of 400 Distance Education students studying in Andhra Pradesh in Open University and school of Distance Education. Each sub-sample was of the size of 200. The sample was considered to be a representative sample of the population of Distance Education learner under BRAOU and School of Distance Education at Andhra University. The population generalisations on Distance Education of this study were attempted from this sample.

Since, three point scale was adopted, the frequency of responses was arrived at for each statement. For convenience of interpretation, the frequencies are converted into percentages.

The data is reported as percentages.

Trend Analysis Procedures

The Trend analysis data as already reported was gathered from various documents, tabulated and trends identified. Wherever necessary a few formulae were evolved and used.

Analysis of Data

Introduction

The evolution of Distance Education System (DES) as an alternative channel for providing higher education and, its gradual development as a parallel stream for providing H.E. raises some questions about its effectiveness in realising the educational goals. The coming one or two decades are most likely to be a period of vast growth and expansion of the DES.

The changing emphasis in the goals of higher education at the national level to meet the challenges of modernisation, development of values, development of secular and democratic attitudes to education, and vocationalisation of higher education makes it imperative for the DES to grow and fall in line with the main educational stream. The DES has to play a proper contributory role in realising goals of higher education and, accordingly strengthen itself. It cannot branch off from the main stream. The legitimate question that needs to be answered is, whether DES performs the role of realising the goals of HE on par with formal structures of education?

With this question as the main objective, this study attempts to identify and evaluate the growth trends in Distance Education in Andhra Pradesh and broadly identify the areas of the Distance Education Programme that need to be strengthened.

Two types of Distance Education Institutions functioning in Andhra Pradesh were identified. One is a well-established SDE functioning in a conventional university environment, the other is an open university, BRAOU.

Trend analysis, faculty interviews, and opinionnaire to the learners were used as tools together data. The data is tabulated, interpreted, conclusions drawn, and generalisations presented in the following pages.

Data of Analysis of Trend

As already pointed out in the previous chapter, trend analysis of DES was attempted in the areas of student enrolment, income and expenditure, successful courses completion, courses offered, research, study centres and multi-media.

1. Student Enrolment—Trends

The following Tables show the over all growth in enrolment, course wise enrolment growth and, enrolment of women in SDE. Table 4.10 shows year wise total enrolment of students and growth trends.

Table 4.10

Total Enrolment Growh Trend SDE

Year	*Total Enrolled*		*Growth*	*Period*
1972-73	355	+	--	--
1973-83	14,469	+	14,204	Ist Decade growth
1983-93	42,476	+	28,007	2nd Decade growth
1993-94	44,620	+	2,156	Yearly growth
1994-95	45,285	+	665	Yearly growth
1995-96	45,639	+	354	Yearly growth
1996-97	46,665	+	1,026	Yearly growth

From Table 4.10, it can be seen that by the end of the first decade the school attained a student strength of around 14,000. During the second decade 1983-93 the enrolment is almost around 42,500. The growth in the enrolment figures show further upward trend and, is currently around 46,000. In all likelihood, with proper expansion the SDE may double up its enrolment by end of this decade. A safe assessment can be that, there will be 50 per cent growth in enrolment.

Table 4.11 shows year wise course wise, enrolment of students in SDE.

Table 4.11

Year Wise, Course Wise Enrolment Trend-SDE

Year	*PUC*	*B.A.*	*B.Com.*	*M.Com.*	*B.Ed.*	*M.Ed.*	*Introductory Course*	*B.Sc.*	*PGDCRS*	*PGDIP*	*M.A. Courses*	*Total*
1972-73	*179	*73	*103	-	-	-	-	-	-	-	-	355
1973-74	*750	**369	339	-	-	-	-	-	-	-	-	1458
1974-75	1278	653	709	-	-	-	-	-	-	-	-	2640
1975-76	1138	838	920	-	-	-	-	-	-	-	-	2896
1976-77	763	848	844	-	-	-	-	-	-	-	-	2455
1977-78	760	993	855	-	-	-	-	-	-	-	-	2608
1978-79	829	1388	951	*734	-	-	-	-	-	-	*369	4271
1979-80	296	2465	1312	1435	-	-	-	-	-	-	712	6220
1980-81	-	4849	1835	1228	550	-	-	-	-	-	643	9105
1981-82	-	7267	2349	923	750	-	-	-	-	-	562	11851
1982-83	-	10318	2828	543	750	-	-	-	-	-	299	14738
1983-84	-	13774	3435	976	750	100	5803	81	254	-	2650	27823
1984-85	-	15620	3640	1030	1250	100	4500**	145	150	-	3338	29773
1985-86	-	17001	3679	1069	754	100	3978	251	111	-	2888	29831
1986-87	-	18204	3831	1220	787	100	1505	263	100	-	3248	29258
1987-88	-	18740	3726	1020	882	100	1055	201	60	-	2744	28528
1988-89	-	22374	4167	1010	704	100	646	276	82	292	2350	32001

(Contd.)

Year	PUC	B.A.	B.Com.	M.Com.	B.Ed.	M.Ed.	Introductory Course	B.Sc.	PGDCRS	PGDIP	M.A. Courses	Total
1989-90	-	24558	3895	1237	723	100	683	433	100	419	3760	35908
1990-91	-	27970	4070	1335	400	100	613	550	100	230	5343	40711
1991-92	-	30933	4471	1852	1205	100	321	615	92	167	3325	43081
1992-93	-	32445	4196	857	557	100	250	504	100	150	3317	42476
1993-94	-	33300	5700	800	580	100	350	600	70	220	2900	44620
1994-95	-	34085	5470	776	450	100	320	740	115	200	3029	45285
1995-96	-	33300	6500	600	350	100	302	577	115	205	2555	44604
1996-97	-	34500	7000	650	420	160	320	500	110	160	2845	46665

* First Year only.

** First and Second Years.

& M.A. Courses include M.A. (Hindi); M.A. (History); M.A. (Politics): M.A. (Sociology): M.A. (Telugu): M.A. (Pad.) and M.A. (English) and M.A. (Economics).

It can be seem from Table 4.11 that there is a fast increasing enrolment in B.A. courses. The commerce courses do not seem to be attracting large number of distance learners compared to the B.A. course. Similarly the B.Sc programme also has limited clientele. A surprising feature is the introductory course meant for Distance Education learners is showing alarming decreasing trend of response from the students. The M.A. courses are attracting a stabilized student population of around 2,500 to 3,000. The P.G. diploma courses are also not getting proper response. The B.Ed. and M.Ed. programmes are governed by Education Common Entrance Test rules of Andhra Pradesh and hence have to admit stipulated number of candidates only.

Table 4.12 shows the trend in enrolment of women students in school of Distance Education.

Table 4.12

Trend in Enrolment of Women in SDE

Year	*Total Enrolment*	*Number of Women*	*% of Women*
1987-88	28,528	10,603	37.2
1992-93	42,476	18,178	42.8
1993-94	44,620	17,326	38.8
1994-95	45,285	17,508	38.7

Source: UNESCO — Bulletin, 1991.
Data reported for years available only.

For the years 1989-90, the percentage of women enrolled in Distance Education at national level was 38.9 per cent and in Andhra Pradesh, it was 33.5 per cent.

The percentage of women enrolments in SDE compares with national figures. Downward trend in enrolment is not evident.

The following Tables 4.13 and 4.14 show the overall growth in enrolment, course-wise enrolment growth, and enrolment of women in open university.

From Table 4.13, it can be seen that the open university's overall enrolment increased by nearly 697 per cent by the year 1996. It is virtually a sevenfold growth from its year of inception.

Table 4.13

Total Enrolment Growth Trend in Open Universty

Year	*Total Enrolment*	*Growth*
1983-84	6,231	—
1984-85	18,699	12,468
1985-86	17,009	(—) 1,690
1986-87	22,795	5,786
1987-88	16,587	(—) 6,208
1988-89	16,827	240
1989-90	19,636	2,809
1990-91	29,547	9,911
1991-92	35,016	4,469
1992-93	36,655	2,637
1993-94	35,149	(—) 1,506
1994-95	34,527	(—) 622
1995-96	41,705	7,178
1996-97	—	—

Source : A.V. R. & R.E., BRAOU, 1995

Table 4.14 shows year wise, course wise enrolment in Open University.

Table 4.14

Course Wise, Year Wise Enrolment Open University

The Academic Year Programme	*U.G. Degree*	*Dip. in Pub. ACC.*	*B.P.R*	*B.L.I.Sc.*	*C.P.F.M.*	*P.G. Degree M.B.A./ M.Sc./M.A.*	*Total*
1983-84	6,231	—	—	—	—	—	6,231
1984-85	11,231	7,468	—	—	—	—	18,699
1985-86	15,702	—	932	375	—	—	17,009
1986-87	19,271	2,414	723	387	—	—	22,795
1987-88	16,303	—	—	284	—	—	16,587
1988-89	16,827	—	—	—	—	—	16,827
1989-90	16,402	54	1040	576	1076		19,636
1990-91	27,458	339	806	450	494	—	29,547
1991-92	32,447	152	578	387	452	—	34,016
1992-93	35,505	—	462	338	350	—	36,655
1993-94	29,283	—	312	354	210	4,990	35,149
1994-95	32,065	—	311	382	1156	613	34,527
1995-96	40,000	—	250	325	—	1,130	41,705

Source : A.VR. & R.C., BRAOU, 1995.

From the above table it can be seen, the growth trend in enrolment indicates that for the years 1987 and 88 it shows reduced trend of enrolment and the years of 1994-95 also show a slight downward trend. But 1996 has shown upward growth. On the whole the undergraduate degrees show an increase in enrolment trend, the P.G. degrees show a downward trend and only course is virtually discontinued. The public relations courses show downward trend. The certificate programme food and nutrition shows un-even trend of students enrolment.

Table 4.15 shows enrolment of women students in open university.

Table 15

Enrolment Pattern of Women (U.G. Courses) Open University

Year	*Total Enrolment*	*Number of Women Enrolled*	*% of Women*
1988-89			
1989-90	16,827	5,436	32
1990-91	16,402	5,408	31
1991-92	27,458	7,518	27
1992-93	32,447	8,708	27
1993-94	35,505	8,181	23
1994-95	29,283	8,097	28
	32,065	8,879	28

Source : A.V.P.R.E. & Students enrolment in U.G. courses BRAOU, 1995.

As, it can be seen from the above table, the percentage of women enrolment in open university is stable and around 28 per cent. This is less than the National and State average.

Table 4.16 shows the data of open university students entering the DES through Non-formal and formal channels.

Table 4.16

Enrolment Entry Channel-Wise Open—University

Year	*Non-Formal*	*Formal*	*Total*
1988-89	11,859 (70.38)	4,990 (29.62)	16,849 (100.00)
1989-90	9,675 (58.91)	6,747 (41.09)	16,422 (100.00)

(*Contd.*)

Year	*Non-Formal*	*Formal*	*Total*
1990-91	18,268 (66.43)	9,230 (33.57)	27,496 (100.00)
1991-92	24,627 (75.90)	7,820 (24.10)	32,447 (100.00)
1992-93	24,602 (69.28)	10,911 (30.72)	35,513 (100.00)
1993-94	18,823 (64.34)	10,432 (35.66)	29,255 (100.00)
1994-95	22,671 (70.68)	9,403 (29.32)	32,074 (100.00)

Figures in the brackets are percentages.

Source: Students enrolment pattern U.G. COURSES — BRAOU, 1995.

No significant trend is evident. On the whole around 65 to 70 per cent of this open University are utilising the non-formal channel, which is an encouraging sign.

Table 4.17 shows occupation wise enrolment pattern of open university learners.

1. From the above table it can be seen that nearly 70 per cent of the open university student population comes under the un-employed category. Under the employed category, in different occupations, a growth trend is evident in agricultural labourers and business people.
2. The enrolment trend for the category of technical personnel, ministrial and clerical people show a downward trend.

Table 4.18 shows medium wise open university enrolment pattern learners in DES.

From the Table 4.18 the trend indicates that the preference of students is the Telugu Medium which, currently stands at around 83 per cent of the student population of the open university.

Table 4.19 shows enrolment pattern of open university learners DES as per special categories i.e., physically handicapped, blind etc.

Table 4.17

Table Showing Enrolment Pattern : Occupation-Wise —Open University

Year	Un-employed	Agrl. Labours	Land Owners	Skilled Workers	Teachers	Nurses	Technical Personnel	Business	Ministe-rial Staff	Political Defence and Others	Total
1988-89	11,532 (68.44)	274 (1.63)	235 (1.39)	39 (0.23)	557 (3.31)	30 (0.18)	415 (2.46)	216 (1.28)	1,532 (9.09)	2,019 (11.98)	16,849 (100.00)
1989-90	11,802 (71.87)	236 (1.44)	163 (0.99)	19 (0.12)	464 (2.83)	8 (0.05)	145 (0.88)	181 (1.10)	548 (3.34)	2,856 (17.39)	16,422 (100.00)
1990-91	21,223 (77.19)	274 (1.00)	365 (1.33)	75 (0.27)	595 (2.16)	24 (0.09)	243 (0.88)	282 (1.03)	738 (2.65)	3,685 (13.40)	27,496 (100.00)
1991-92	23,982 (73.91)	594 (1.83)	518 (1.60)	73 (0.22)	528 (1.63)	25 (0.08)	135 (0.42)	438 (1.35)	730 (2.27)	5,417 (16.69)	32,447 (100.00)
1992-93	27,729 (78.08)	721 (2.03)	408 (1.15)	32 (0.09)	398 (1.12)	19 (0.05)	101 (0.28)	395 (1.11)	396 (1.12)	5,314 (14.96)	35,513 (100.00)
1993-94	19,918 (68.08)	1,923 (6.57)	769 (2.63)	117 (0.40)	551 (1.88)	11 (0.04)	75 (0.26)	1,008 (3.45)	277 (0.95)	4,606 (15.74)	29,255 (100.00)
1994-95	22,639 (70.58)	1,883 (5.87)	698 (2.18)	131 (0.41)	450 (1.40)	32 (0.10)	36 (0.11)	807 (2.52)	200 (0.62)	5,198 (16.24)	32,074 (100.00)

Figures in the brackets are percentages.
Source : Students employment pattern U.G. COURSES-BRAOU-1995.

Table 4.18

Table Showing Enrolment Pattern-Medium Wise-Open University

Year	*Telugu*	*Hindi*	*Urdu*	*Additional English*	*Total*
1988-89	14,633 (86.65)	1,797 (10.67)	419 (2.49)	0* (0.00)	16,849 (100.00)
1989-90	14,203 (86.49)	1,848 (11.25)	371 (2.26)	0* (0.00)	16,422 (100.00)
1990-91	23,646 (86.00)	3,183 (11.58)	667 (2.43)	0* (0.00)	27,496 (100.00)
1991-92	28,453 (87.69)	3,244 (10.00)	750 (2.31)	0* (0.00)	32,447 (100.00)
1992-93	31,393 (88.40)	3,204 (9.02)	570 (1.61)	340 (0.97)	35,513 (100.00)
1993-94	24,537 (83.87)	2,277 (7.78)	443 (1.51)	1998 (6.83)	29,255 (100.00)
1994-95	26,987 (84.14)	2,512 (7.83)	435 (1.36)	2140 (6.67)	32,074 (100.00)

Figures in the brackets are percentages.
Source : Student Enrolment pattern U.G. COURSES-BRAOU-1995.

Table 4.19

Enrolment Pattern Special Categories Wise-Open University

Year	*Physically Handicapped*	*Blind*	*Ex-Service*	*Prisoners*	*Total*
1988-89	38 (26.95)	17 (12.06)	45 (31.91)	41 (29.08)	141 (100.00)
1989-90	39 (44.83)	16 (18.39)	20 (22.99)	12 (13.79)	87 (100.00)
1990-91	88 (48.09)	24 (13.11)	44 (24.04)	27 (14.75)	183 (100.00)
1991-92	101 (49.03)	13 (6.31)	53 (25.73)	39 (18.93)	206 (100.00)
1992-93	109 (46.38)	35 (14.89)	56 (23.83)	35 (14.89)	235 (100.00)
1993-94	45 (42.45)	4 (3.77)	18 (16.98)	39 (36.79)	106 (100.00)
1994-95	40 (36.36)	13 (11.82)	4 (3.64)	53 (48.18)	110 (100.00)

Figures in the brackets are percentages.
Source : Students enrolment pattern U.G. COURSE-BRAOU-1995.

From the above table, figurwise, there is no extraordinary increase in the number of students enrolled under special categories over the years. No significant trend is present. This may be because proper facilities are not provided for physically handicapped and visually handicapped learners of DE.

2. Income and Expenditure Growth Trends

Tables 4.20 and 4.21 show the income and expenditure data and expenditure per student of the SDE.

Table 20

Year Wise Income and Expenditure-SDE

Year	*Income*	*Expenditure*	*Credit Balance*
1987-88	198.09	178.27	19.82
1988-89	216.28	200.89	15.40
1989-90	297.66	265.08	32.57
1990-91	351.44	351.41	0.03
1991-92	453.82	451.25	2.56
1992-93	349.29	348.86	0.43
1993-94	326.77	325.84	0.97
1994-95	427.64	427.02	0.62
1995-96	527.82	527.34	0.47
1996-97	569.98	569.40	0.58

Source: Budget Reports—Andhra University—Figures in Lakhs of Rupees.

It can be seen from Table 4.20 that there is a steady growth in the income an Expenditure of SDE. The gap between the income and expenditure is reduced from the year 1990. The institution evidently is not running on loss.

Table 4.21 shows average annual expenditure per student from the year 1987-88 to 1996-97. The following formula was used. Average expenditure per student = Total annual expenditure Total enrolment for the year.

It can be seen from the below table that the expenditure per student doubled during the decade. The current figures about cost per student in various Distance Education Institutions in the country are not available.

Table 4.21

Annual Expenditure Per Student — SDE

Year	*Total Enrolment*	*Total Annual Expenditure (in Rupees)*	*Average Expenditure Per Student (In Rupees)*
1987-88	28,528	1,78,27,043	625
1988-89	32,001	2,00,87,575	628
1989-90	35,908	2,65,08,650	738
1990-91	40,711	3,51,25,961	863
1991-92	42,087	4,51,25,961	1072
1992-93	42,476	3,48,86,400	821
1993-94	44,620	3,25,80,000	730
1994-95	45,285	4,27,02,000	943
1995-96	46,639	5,27,34,827	1130
1996-97	46,665	5,69,40,000	1220

Source : Budget Reports - Andhra University.

Tables 4.22 and 4.23 shows the income and expenditure data and expenditure per student of the open university.

Table 4.22

Year Wise Income and Expenditure — Open University

Year	*Income (A)*	*Expenditure(B)*	*(A—B) Total*
1983-84	33.94	33.97	(—) 0.03
1984-85	200.44	173.31	27.13
1985-86	312.56	204.31	108.25
1986-87	278.29	255.31	22.98
1987-88	383.68	203.95	179.73
1988-89	303.27	287.60	15.67
1989-90	357.19	320.27	36.92
1990-91	428.09	373.68	54.41
1991-92	481.81	500.97	(—) 19.16
1992-93	596.55	563.46	33.09
1993-94	--	--	--
1994-95	1243.50	1157.40	86.01
1995-96	1043.44	895.15	148.29
1996-97	1372.11	1340.77	31.34

Source : Funding of DEA Case Study of an OU, Budget Report — BRAOU.

From the above table, it can be seen that there is a steady increase in the income and expenditure aspects of the open university. From the years 1994-95 onwards the income of open university has virtually doubled. Excepting for two years 1983-84 and 1991-92 the open university has not shown deficit. The income and expenditure differences seem to indicate that the funds are not utilized fully.

Table 4.23 shows Annual Expenditure per student in Open University.

Table 4.23

Annual Expenditure Per Student - Open University

Year	*Total Enrolment*	*Total Expenditure (In Lakhs of Rupees)*	*Expenditure Per Student (In Rupees)*
1983-84	6,231	33.97	545
1984-85	18,699	173.31	926
1985-86	17,009	204.31	1,201
1986-87	22,795	255.31	1,120
1987-88	16,587	203.95	1,229
1988-89	16,827	287.60	1,709
1989-90	19,636	320.27	1,631
1990-91	29,547	373.68	1,264
1991-92	34,016	500.97	1,472
1992-93	36,655	563.46	1,537
1993-94	35,149	—	—
1994-95	34,527	1157.40	3,352
1995-96	41,705	895.15	2,146

Source : Funding of D.E.A case study of an O.U., Budget Reports — BRAOU.

From the above table, it can be seen that in the open university the annual expenditure per student has doubled during the last ten years. And now it is currently around, Rupees two thousand.

3. Successful Course Completion by DE Learners

The following tables show the trends in successful course completion by students in the SDE and OU.

Table 4.24 shows successful course completion by students of SDE over years.

Table 4.24

Successful Course Completion by DE Learners

Year	*Total Enrolment*	*Number Appeared for Exam.*	*Total No. Passed*	*Overall % of Pass c/b x 100*	*Appearing for Examination b/a x 100*	*Overall Success Rate c/a x 100*
1988	28,528	6,154	2,004	30.7%	21.6	7.08
1990	35,908	2,787	774	27.7%	7.8	2.1
1991	40,711	5,623	2,551	45.4%	15.8	6.3
1992	42,087	6,591	3,191	48.4%	13.8	7.6
1994	44,620	7,819	2,973	38.0%	17.5	6.7
1995	45,285	8,588	3,324	38.7%	18.9	7.3
1996 1997	DATA NOT AVAILABLE					

Source : Annual Report - Andhra Pradesh.

From the above table it can be observed that the overall success rate of students of this S.D.E. is less than eight per cent. Similarly the percentage of students completing the formalities and coming to the stage of taking the examinations is less than nineteen per cent. The overall pass rate of the students taking the examination is between 38 to 40 per cent.

Table shows successful course completion of students of Open University.

Table 4.25

Successful Course Completion of Students OU

Year	*Total Enrolment*	*Total Pass*	*Overall Success %*
1986-87	22,795	1,491	6.5
1987-88	16,587	2,015	12.1
1988-89	16,827	2,965	17.6
1989-90	19,636	4,155	21.2
1990-91	29,547	4,882	16.5
1991-92	34,016	—	—
1992-93	36,655	3,434	9.4
1993-94	35,149	—	—
1994-95	34,527	—	—
1995-96	41,705	—	—

Source : Hand Book, BRAOU, 1993-94.

From Table 4.25, it can be observed that the over all success rate of students of open university is ranging between 6 per cent to 21 per cent over different years.

The latest figures were not available. Between 1987 and 1991 the students success rate is comparatively better than, the success rate of students of SDE.

4. Growth in Number of Disciplines

Tables 4.26 and 4.27 show the number of courses offered by the SDE & OU and their growth in number in the previous years.

Table 4.26

Growth in Number of Disciplines — SDE

Year	*Courses Started*	*No. of Courses Run During the Year*
1972-73	PUC., B.A., B.Com.	3
1977-78	PUC., B.A., B.Com.	3
1978-79	M.A., M.Com., also introduced	5
1980-81	B.Ed., introduced & PUC discontinued	5
1983-84	M.Ed. Introductory Courses B.Sc., M.A. (Eng.) M.A. (PAD)	11
1988-89	One Year P.G. Diploma	12
1989-90	New M.A. Courses	13

Source : Annual Reports — Andhra University.

Table 4.27

Course Description — OU

Sl. No.	*Name of the Courses*		*No. of Courses*
1.	Under Graduate Courses	B.A., B.Sc., B.Com.	3
2.	Post-Graduate Courses	M.A.(Pub.Adm.), M.A. (Politics) M.A.(Economics), M.A.(History) M.B.A. and M.Sc. Mathematics	6
3.	Bachelor Courses	Public Relations (BPR) Library and Information Science (B.L.I.Sc.)	2

(*Contd.*)

Sl. No.	*Name of the Courses*		*No. of Courses*
4.	Diploma Courses	Dip. in Public Accounting Dip. in Business Finance Dip. in Marketing Management	3
5.	Certificate Courses	Food & Nutrition (C PFN)	1
6.	Research Courses	Ph.D. & M.Phil	2
		Total	17

Source : A.V.P. & R. E, BRAOU — 1995.

From Tables 4.26 and 4.27 it is observed that there is a gradual growth in number of courses offered by these two Distance Education Institutions. The medium of instruction offered and the study materials is in two languages that is English and Telugu.

5. Growth in Research

I. The following are the findings about research facilities in school of Distance Education.

(a) Facilities for the Distance Education learner to research degrees like: M.Phil: Ph.D., Provisions are not made for sophisticated — research programmes.

(b) Under the guidance of regular university staff, the faculty is permitted to acquire research qualifications, like-M.Phil and Ph.D. From out of the core faculty to twenty eight, twenty two have acquired Ph.D. Degrees.

(c) Though the faculty is qualified to direct research, arrangements are not yet made to offer M.Phil and Ph.D. Degrees to students.

(d) Data is not available about research publications of the faculty.

Source : Status Report — A.U.

Table 28 shows research degrees awarded by Open University.

Table 4.28

Table Showing Growth in Research—M.Phil. Degree Awarded in OU

Sl. No.	*Area of Specialisation (Branch)*	*No. of M.Phil Degrees Awarded*
1.	Commerce	9
2.	Economics	5
3.	Political Science & Public Administration	5
		19

Source : Hand Book, BRAOU — 1993-94.

The Open University is providing research facilities for students of Distance Education. It can be seen from the above table, that it is awarding M.Phil degrees. The university is having facilities for Ph.D programme also. The data regarding the number of Ph.D degrees awarded was not available.

6. Growth in Study Centres

Table 4.29 shows Growth trends in study centres in School of Distance Education.

Table 4.29

Growth in Study Centres — SDE

Year	*No. of Courses Started in that Year*	*Total During the Year*
1986-87	8	8
1988	3	11
1989	4	15
1990	4	19
1991	3	22
1992	1	23
1993	2	25
1994	1	26
1995	1	27
1996	2	29
1997	3	32

Source : Status Report — A.U., 1997.

As seen from the above table.

(a) There is four-fold increase in the number of study centres in SDE with in a decade.

(b) From the reports it is found that study centres are mainly located with in the university area and Andhra coastal districts of Andhra Pradesh.

(c) Study centres are also located at state and National capitals and in a neighbouring country Mauritius.

Table 4.30 shows Growth trends in Study Centres in Open University.

Table 4.30

Growth in Study Centres — OU

Year	*Total in Existing During that Year*
1983	26
1984	30
1985	30
1986	57
1987	57
1988	57
1989	58
1990	60
1991	74
1992	85
1993	92
1994	92
1995	100
1996	107
1997	107

1. As seen from the above table, there is a four fold increase in the number of study centres in the open university from the year of inception to 1997.
2. Besides, there are twelve post graduate study centres.
3. The study centres are located and distributed geographically in the entire state.

Source : 1. Hand Book, BRAOU, 1993-94.
2. ENADU — 27-4-97, Interview with V.C.

7. Growth of Multi-Media

Growth in Multi Media-SDE, AU

(a) From its inception in 1972 till 1996 this SDE is predominantly dependent upon providing print material to the learner. There were periodic revisions and improvement of the study materials provided to the Distance Education learners.

(b) The school has initiated steps for the process of converting into Distance Education mode.

(c) Attempts are being made to convert the study material into self instructional material (SIM).

(d) The school has started the Tele-conference Net-work classes for its students.

(i) An audio cassette is being issued to develop students communication skills.

(ii) Video lessons are not available at present.

Growth of Multi-Media—BROU

Table 4.27 shows multimedia developed by Open University over the years.

Table 4.31

Programme Production Achievement During 1983-84 to 1995-96 — OU

Academic Year	Total		
	R	A	*V*
1983-84	127	—	03
1984-85	228	22	24
1985-86	268	24	36
1986-87	221	54	24
1987-88	129	55	11
1988-89	59	43	09
1989-90	32	22	08
1990-91	29	08	07
1991-92	22	04	08
1992-93	25	—	18
1993-94	144	—	30
1994-95	18	—	—
1995-96	12	02	—

Source : A.V.R. & R. C, BRAOU, 1995.

R = Programmes for Radio Broadcast.

A = Audio Programmes.

V = Video Programmes.

From Table 4.31, it can be observed the rate of multi media programme production achievement in OU shows a downward trend. Since, 1991-92 the audio and video programme production restricted in number, except in the year 1993-94, the,radio programme production also shows a similar trend. It is apparent that, currently enough emphasis is not given in open university to multi-media package production.

Findings of the Study

From the interpretation of data of the institutions viz., Open University and SDE, the following trends are evident in the DES of Andhra Pradesh.

1. Enrolment Trends

1. There appears to be an upward enrolment trend in this DES. It is enough evidence to conclude that more and more students in this state are getting attracted to the DES.
2. The DES is also serving the cause of women education. On an average 28 to 38 per cent of the Distance Education learners are women.
3. The non-formal entry channel for higher education is preferred by the learners of the system.
4. The turn over of students in DES is mainly in undergraduate courses, and that too in B.A. course.
5. The preference of Distance Education learner appears to be to learn in their mother tongue i.e., Telugu.
6. But for a few courses almost all the courses offered by the DES are attracting learners.

2. Economic Trends

1. Analysis of the available data leads to the conclusion that the DES is economically sound.
2. In the DES, the expenditure per student has doubled in the last ten years. Along, with income through students tuition fees, the DES is also receiving funds from the National agencies of higher education viz: — UGC and Higher Education Council. That is why, the DES is able to spend more money on the Distance Education Learner.

3. Trends in Successful Course Completion of Students

1. In terms of the overall intake of the students into the DES, the overall success rate of the students appears to be low. In one institution it war around seven per cent and the other around fifteen per cent.
2. It is clear that the wastage and stagnation of students in the DES is quite high.
3. The DES is not making efforts to study this problem of

wastage and stagnation. The reports and data made available did not consider this important aspect which affects the success rate immensely.

4. While the enrolment figures are raising, the percentage of students appearing for examinations is virtually stable.

4. Growth Trend in Number of Disciplines

1. The DES is offering 15 to 19 courses at present.
2. Starting with foundation course for the Distance Education learner, facilities are provided for acquiring research degrees also.
3. Vocational courses and short duration certificate and Diploma courses are also provided in the DES.
4. Education in various disciplines are provided. Ex: Languages, Arts and Sciences.
5. The DES shows the trend of introduction of new courses periodically.

5. Growth Trends in Research

1. The DES in Andhra Pradesh has the facilities and qualified staff for conducting research.
2. In the immediate future, the system can have the proper infrastructure for providing research facilities to Distance Education learners.

6. Growth Trends in Study Centres

1. The DES is providing enough study centres for DE learners.
2. The open University has started more study centres than the SDE.

7. Growth Trends in Multi-Media

1. The DES is giving increased emphasis to the use of multi-media.
2. Attempts are being made to use the television net works, tele conferences and radio broad castings to educate the learners.
3. But, the main emphasis of the DES is on study material provided to the learner.

4. The Self Instructional Material (SIM) for each course is being prepared, evaluated and introduced.

Interview Report-Faculty of Distance Education System

An unstructured interview schedule consisting of nine questions was prepared and fifteen of the faculty members of each institution were interviewed. The duration of each interview ranged from 20 to 45 minutes. The respondents were co-operative and substantiated their opinions and suggestions.

Summary of Opinions — Interview Schedule

1. The interview sample unanimously opined that the DES in the State is helping in realisation of the goals of higher education. They are of the opinion that along with the acquisition of qualifications, the Distance Education learner is helped to improve his knowledge skills, which help him in understanding the various social, local, national and international issues. The faculty is of the opinion that the DES in the State posesses the main characteristics of flexibility and accessibility to learner.
2. When asked about the need for expansion of Distance Education Institutions in the State, they felt that there is no need for starting more and more Distance Education Institutions in the State because, there is already one open University and five schools of Distance Education catering to the learners.
3. The faculty unanimously opined that they have enough autonomy in the DES. They reported that each faculty is independent.
4. While most of them admitted that there is a need for redesigning of courses in DES, the suggestions in this direction were varied.

They are:

(a) All the Directors and majority of the teaching personnel, in the interview sample felt, that there is a need for job-oriented courses.

(b) Three of the Directors and one Assistant Director spoke at length, on the need for designing courses suitable to needs of the local environment. They suggested, that the educational needs of a particular area may be surveyed.

For example: Distance learners in tobacco growing areas, Distance learners around seashore etc.

(c) One of the Directors had a interesting proposal for incorporation into the Distance Education. He strongly felt, the need for introduction of skill oriented courses. He was of the opinion that, the Distance Education learners can be trained to acquire some useful skills, which may enable them to earn their livelihood. He suggested, that skill oriented courses like auto repairing, motor repairing, T.V. and Radio mechanism can be introduced through DES. He felt, it is possible to prepare the self-learning materials and suggested that the mass media can be very effectively used.

5. The faculty reported that the DES is playing proper role in producing and training teachers for the educational system because, a number of DE students are entering into teaching profession.
6. They expressed the need for strengthening the research in DES. They opined that, since the faculty is fully qualified to guide research students for M.Phil and Ph.D., proper arrangements can be made at the earliest to introduce research degrees. They also expressed a strong opinion that the DES in the state is mature enough to introduce the research degrees for Distance Education learners.
7. When asked about the areas of DES that need to be strengthened, their opinions mainly centered around Student Support Services (SSS) and study centres.

They all felt that SSS and study centres are the backbone of the DES. Every care should be taken continuously to strengthen them, maintain quality and, meet clientele requirements.

There were some suggestions to improve the student support services and study centres. They are :

(i) Timely dispatch of study material.

(ii) Improving facilities in the existing study centres, specially the library facilities.

(iii) Majority of the interview sample felt, that there is a need to monitor the DES because of the different agencies providing higher education and the need for uniformity in the system. They suggested that an apex body will serve a useful purpose. Some of them suggested that all institutions in the country providing Distance Education should be brought under the control of a single apex body to be called as National apex body of Distance Education.

(iv) The faculty opined that in the DES, the learner has enough mobility. They have the freedom to choose courses, choose the study centre and have proper accessibility. They were not in favour of giving freedom to the learner to move from one open university to another open university in the middle of a course.

(v) Some of them suggested that each state should have an open university to act as the state apex body for Distance Education and all the Distance Education Institutions in that state can be attached to the state apex body.

Findings of the Faculty Opinions — Interview Reports

It is concluded that the faculty of the DES in the Andhra Pradesh who are at the helm of affairs hold concrete, positive and futuristic opinions about the effectiveness of the DES and, the areas that need to be strengthened to make it more effective to realise the goals of higher education.

(i) In their opinion the DES is as effective as the conventional system in providing higher education.

(ii) The need for consolidation and expansion of the facilities to meet the future demands for higher education through DES is there.

(iii) There is enough of autonomy in DES.

(iv) There is a need for redesigning of courses in the DES, in order to meet the growing demands of the specialisation and modernisation of the curricula.

(v) There were no suggestions regarding reforms in the evaluation procedures in the DES.

(vi) The DES is also meeting the need of providing teachers for the education system.

(vii)There is a need for as apex body to monitor and coordinate the DES in Andhra Pradesh.

Opinions of Learners Towards the Distance Education System

The following data shows the trend of responses of this sample of Distance Education learners of two institutions towards the DES. The trend is reported as percentage frequencies on a three point scale.

As one aspect of the study is to evaluate the effectiveness of the system through learners opinions, a total sample of 400 learners of the DES were contacted by adopting quota sampling.

The learners were asked to express their opinions on the following areas:

(i) The overall facilities in the system.

(ii) Courses, curriculum and evaluation.

(iii) Student Support Services (SSS).

(iv) The difficulties faced by them in the system.

(v) Their opinions about the educational goals realised.

Opinionnaire Data of Learners of Distance Education System

As already reported the sample was drawn from two institutions. On the three point scaling that was adopted, the frequency of sample responses were tabulated. The original frequencies are given in appendix. For the purpose of convenience of comparision and interpretation, the frequencies are reported as percentages. The percentages are rounded up to the nearest integer.

Table 4.32 shows the opinions of Distance Education learners towards overall facilities in the DES.

Table 4.32

Learners Opinions of Over All Facilities

Sl. No.	*Statements*	*Opinions in Percentages*		
		Agree	*Undecided*	*Disagree*
1.	Distance Education Universities/ Directorates are accessible to students in seeking information	78	17	5
2.	The admission procedures are systematic	70	20	10

(Contd.)

Sl. No	*Statements*	*Opinions in Percentages*		
		Agree	*Undecided*	*Disagree*
3.	The facilities at study centres are very useful to students	50	37	13
4.	The infrastructure facilities (Building, Classrooms, Library, P.C.P. Centers etc.) offer adequate accommodation	82	12	6

As seen from the above table eighty two per cent of the sample are of the opinion, that the infrastructure facilities provided to students have adequate accommodation.

Seventy eight per cent of the sample admit that the Distance Education universities and Directorates are accessible to students in seeking information.

Seventy per cent are of the opinion that the admission procedures are systematic.

Only fifty per cent feel that the facilities at study centres are very useful to students.

Table 4.33 shows the opinions of Distance Education Learners towards curriculum, courses and evaluation in the system.

Table 4.33

Learners Opinions Towards Curriculum, Courses and Evaluation in DES

Sl. No.	*Statement*	*Opinions in Percentages*		
		Agree	*Undecided*	*Disagree*
1.	There is a need to introduce more courses	77	18	5
2.	There is a need of continuous evaluation in courses	30	48	22
3.	Evaluation procedures should be improved	73	25	2
4.	Courses are suitable to the needs of the students	73	21	6
5.	More job oriented courses should be introduced	83	14	3
6.	The Distance Education Curriculum is very relevant to student needs	31	44	25
7.	There is a need for introducing teacher education courses like B.Ed.	33	45	22

As can be seen from Table 4.33, eighty three per cent of the sample is of the opinion that more job oriented courses are to be introduced.

Seventy seven per cent opined that there is a need to introduce more courses. Seventy three per cent felt that the courses are suitable to the needs of the students.

Seventy three per cent expressed the opinion that the evaluation procedures should be improved.

Regarding the need of continuous evaluation in the courses, the opinions are equally distributed.

Once again the opinions were almost evenly divided about, whether the DES is offering enough number of courses and the need for introducing teacher training courses.

Table 4.34 shows opinions of Distance Education learners towards Students Support Services (SSS)

Table 4.34

Opinions of Distance Education Learners Towards SSS in DES

(Opinions in Percentages)

Sl. No.	*Statement*	*A*	*U*	*D*
1.	Course material is usually supplied in time	60	23	17
2.	Course material is covering the entire syllabus	60	23	17
3.	Assignment approach is properly followed	61	21	18
4.	Assignment is given in terms of instructional goals	60	23	17
5.	Study centres are quite useful	60	21	19
6.	Counselling timings are suitable to students	80	16	04
7.	The quality of counselling is satisfactory	58	27	15
8.	Personal Contact Programme (PCP) are beneficial to students	55	36	09
9.	The teacher-student rapport during P.C.P. is satisfactory	78	20	02
10.	P.C.P. dates are convenient to students	65	24	11
11.	Multi-media (Radio Broadcasts, Audio Cassettes, Video Cassettes and T.V. are used effectively	61	20	19

As seen from the table eighty percent of the sample is of the opinion, that the study centres are quite useful.

Seventy eight per cent of the students opined that PCP is useful to students.

Sixty five per cent felt that the teacher student rapport during PCP is satisfactory.

Sixty one per cent students are of the opinion that PCP dates are convenient to students.

Nearly sixty per cent of the students expressed the following opinions:

(a) Course material is usually supplied in time and is covering the entire syllabus.

(b) Assignment approach is being followed and is given in terms of instructional goals.

(c) One of the most significant opinions is, they report that the multi-media is not used properly.

Table 4.35 Shows the opinions of Distance Education learners about the goals of higher education being realised by the DES.

Table 4.35

Opinions of Distance Education Learners About Goals of Higher Education Being Realised in DES

(Opinions in Percentages)

Sl. No.	*Statement*	*A*	*U*	*D*
1.	Distance Education approach helps in understanding social issues in the country	83	15	2
2.	Distance Education gives opportunity to understand economic issues in the country	39	51	10
3.	Enables me to understand moral and spiritual issues faced by mankind	34	20	46
4.	Allows me to understand Indian culture	34	35	31
5.	Gives scope to know cultural issues in the world	35	37	28
6.	Distance Education promotes the acquisition of specialised knowledge	65	15	20
7.	Develops specialised professional knowledge	4	22	74
8.	Helps to contribute to National Development	78	20	2
9.	Distance Education guides students to opt for teaching profession	80	18	2

Eighty three per cent of the sample opined, that the DES helps in understanding social issues.

Eighty per cent reported that the DES, if necessary helps them to be ready to be a teacher.

Seventy eight per cent reported that the DES makes them ready to contribute to national development.

Sixty five per cent are of the opinion that it makes them acquire specialised knowledge. But seventy four percent of the sample are of the opinion that the DES does not develop specialised skills.

For the rest of the goals, the opinions appear to be equally divided.

Table 4.36 shows difficulties faced by the learners in DES.

Table 4.36

Difficulties Faced by Learners in DES

(Opinions in Percentages)

Sl. No.	*Statement*	*No. Difficulty*	*U*	*Difficulty*
1.	Admission Procedures	98	2	—
2.	Payment of fees	85	13	2
3.	Eligibility certification	89	7	4
4.	Learning material	89	7	4
5.	Information about P.C.P.	90	5	5
6.	Attending P.C.P.	88	9	3
7.	Library services	5	22	73
8.	Counselling by Counsellors	70	23	7
9.	Examination dates	45	7	48
10.	Publication of examination results	28	22	50

It can be seen that seventy three per cent of the sample reported difficulty regarding acquiring the library books in the DES.

Fifty per cent reported difficulty in receiving information about examination results; while forty eight per cent admitted difficulty in knowing the dates of examination. But forty five per cent hold the opposite view about knowing dates of examination.

Opinions of Learners — Findings

The following conclusions about the DES in Andhra Pradesh are drawn on the basis of learner opinions.

(i) The DES is accessible to the learners.

(ii) The infrastructure facilities of the DES are satisfactory.

(iii) More number of courses with Job orientation have to be introduced.

(iv) The present courses are suitable to the present needs.

(v) Evaluation procedures in the DES need improvement.

(vi) The teacher student rapport is good.

(vii) The PCPs are useful to the students.

(viii) Counselling is good.

(ix) The DES is helping the learners in understanding social issues and makes them ready to contribute to National development.

(x) The DES is able to prepare teachers needed by the educational system.

As far as the learner opinions are concerned the following are the negative aspects of the Distance Education System.

(i) They feel that, the education they are receiving is not helping in developing specialised knowledge.

(ii) The learner has difficulty with regard to the library books.

(iii) He has a problem in receiving information about examination dates and results.

Discussion and Suggestions

The aim of this investigation was to evaluate the effectiveness of DES in Andhra Pradesh. Three different sources of data were used viz., Institutional data, faculty opinions and learners opinions.

The reference points for evaluating the system were:

1. Its effectiveness in realising the goals of higher education as viewed by faculty and learners.
2. Overall areas that need strengthening, in terms of National Policy of Education (1986) recommendations as identified by faculty.
3. The existing strengths and weaknesses of the system as viewed and identified by the learner.

On the basis of the findings, it is concluded that the DES is functioning effectively in the state of Andhra Pradesh.

As evident from the faculty and learner opinions, the system is providing to the realisation of the knowledge objective, helping the learners to understand social issues, and enabling them to contribute to national development. It is also evident that the Distance Education approach is providing teachers for the educational system.

The DES in Andhra Pradesh is showing healthy growth trends as was evident from the findings of the trend data. The system is economically sound. Student expenditure per year is satisfactory. The system has the necessary infrastructural facilities.

There is a gradual increase of student enrolment in this system.

The DES evidently has the capacity to handle large student populations. This can be seen from the current annual enrolment of nearly 45,000 in each of the institutes studied. The administrators of Distance Education have the plans and confidence to handle even higher student enrolments of up to 75,000 in each institution in future. The trends of the demand for enrolment indicate that in the coming ten years the student enrolment into the DES is likely to increase two fold.

Evidently, the DES is playing its effective role in the field of women's' education. Nearly thirty per cent of the Distance Education learners are women students. From the view point of flexibility and accessibility the DES has gone closer and closer to learners, as nearly seventy per cent of those that want to enter the Distance Education stream of higher education are choosing the non-formal entry route.

In line with the National Policy of Education that the medium of instruction is to be in mother tongue, the DES is able to cater to the students who want the mother tongue as the medium of learning. As a matter of fact, eighty per cent of the Distance Education learners are receiving education in their mother tongue i.e., Telugu.

The DES is offering a number of courses in various disciplines. The courses offered range from the foundation courses to research degrees. There is a gradual growth in the number of courses being offered by the DES. At present, DES has also recognised the need for providing vocational courses, short duration diploma courses, and is offering these courses in areas like Library science, Business Management, Nutrition etc.

The DES is also contributing much in the area of research. The faculty at the helm of affairs is highly qualified and willing to take up the research function also.

There is a steady growth in the number of study centres. As part of the Student Support Services, the study centres are playing a key role in the DES.

Like any other modern education system, the Distance Education approach also has to depend on multi-media. Compared to the earlier years, now a days DES in A.P., is giving increased emphasis to the use of multi-media. Attempts are being made to liberally use television net works and radio broad casting. The system is producing some audio, and video cassettes for the use of learners, But, it is observed in this study that the systematic usage of multi-media in the DES is not seriously viewed by the producers and consumers.

The system is efficiently producing and supplying the study materials to the learners. The study material is following the pattern of self instructional material with inbuilt self evaluation approach.

But, the trends in overall, success rate of students of DES need detailed and thorough investigation. In every educational system there is wastage and stagnation. DES is no exception to this. The overall trends in results indicate that the success rate of the students is low. Between seven to fifteen per cent of the students are passing out successfully.

The student profile shows, that nearly seventy per cent are opting for Bachelor of Arts degree in Telugu medium. As already reported, nearly seventy per cent of the students are entering through non-formal stream. This is a large chunk of the student population in the DES and, may be, it is the reason why the results are dismal.

This investigator strongly opines that wastage and stagnation studies on DES in Andhra Pradesh will serve a useful purpose to give guide lines to make the system more effective.

The NPE (1986) has made various recommendations to strengthen the institutions of higher education. DES has evolved as a parallel approach to higher education by adopting the Distance mode of learning and, the inherent characteristics of flexibility and accessibility. System wise, a direct comparision of conventional higher educational system with the DES cannot be made. The Distance Education is latest innovation in the field of education. The clientele are all adults from different walks of life and self motivated. Of late, the Distance Education is serving more to the cause of higher education.

The faculty of the DES who are the helm of affairs, expressed a range of opinions on what areas are to be strengthened.

One important observation was, that DES is as effective as

the conventional system in realising the aims of higher education. This shows a confidence in themselves and confidence about the effectiveness of the system.

The system needs expansion and consolidation of the facilities to meet the future demands for higher education. The DES requires modernisation of the curricula to meet the growing demands of specialisation. There is a need for redesigning of the courses. Substantiating the faculty opinions, this is also evident in view of the limited number of conventional degrees that are being offered by the system. There is also a demand for job-oriented courses from learners.

More than autonomy, what the system needs is better co-ordination. Need for autonomy was not expressed by the faculty. The DES needs an apex body to monitor and co-ordinate the system. This is necessary in view of the need for uniform curricula, uniform courses, and common rules and regulations.

The learners experience in this educational system was another reference point for evaluating its effectiveness.

The learners of DES in A.P., make the following positive assessment. From their view point :

1. The system is accessible.
2. Infrastructural facilities are adequate.
3. Courses are suitable to the present needs.
4. Good teacher-student rapport exists.
5. Personal contact programmes are useful.
6. Good counselling is given.
7. The learner requirements are:
   (a) More number of courses with job-orientation are needed.
   (b) Improvement in evaluation procedures is desirable.
   (c) The learner problems are:
      (i) Difficulty is there with regard to the availability of library books.
      (ii) Difficulty in receiving information about examination dates and results in felt.

The learner evaluated the effectiveness of DES in realising the goals of higher education as follows:

1. The system is helping in understanding social issues.
2. The system is contributing for national development.
3. The system is able to prepare teachers needed by the educational system in India.
4. The system is not effective in helping them to develop specialised knowledge.

Suggestions

The following suggestions may be considered to make the DES more effective.

1. Region wise surveys of needs of learners aspiring to enter into the DES will result in useful data to plan job-oriented courses.
2. Each institution in the DES is adopting its own multi-media approach. Common multi-media packages for use of the Distance Education learners, irrespective of the institution in which they are studying, will serve a useful purpose.
3. Each institution must make a honest and detailed study of wastage and stagnation. This wastage and stagnation data may be taken as the basis for SSS, PCP and other important aspects. This data will be very helpful in planning to make the Distance Education approach more effective.
4. An apex body to monitor DES is extremely desirable and urgently needed.
5. The DES is mainly self funding. Of late, it is receiving substantial grants and funds from UGC and the State Government. In the conventional system, there are certain provisions for the students community on the basis of the reservations and economic status. The extension of a similar facility to the student of Distance Education will serve a useful purpose of social justice in Indian context.
6. Development of a holistic model for evaluating the effectiveness of DES periodically is needed. This type of model can be simple diagnostic in nature. It can enable the authorities to implement the recommendations which will be specific and concrete. This evaluation programme has to evolve simple and well defined tools.

The type of tools that can be used here are:

(a) Institutional environment.

(b) System co-ordination.

(c) Attitudes of faculty and learners.

(d) Growth trends in the system.

(e) Basic cost analysis.

(f) Public opinions.

A team of trained objective investigators can be made to conduct this type of educational audit every year, make recommendations for improving system efficiency and bring out a generalised picture of the effectiveness of the system from time to time. This kind of continuous cross sectional studies can be subjected to meta analysis for validity of the recommendations.

7. Science education through Distance Mode appears to be weak in the DES of Andhra Pradesh. No doubt social sciences are much preferred by the DE learners and there is a heavy demand for arts courses. In order, to meet the demand for science education through DE approach, some improvements are necessary.

Teaching of Science needs well equipped laboratories. The conventional universities and degree colleges have well organised laboratories meant for teaching and research programmes. But, the DE Institutions in Andhra Pradesh are still in the stage of organising themselves for teaching science.

keeping in view, the limitations of Distance learners, the following suggestions to improve science education for DES are made.

(a) Since the learner cannot come to the institution quite often, there is a need to introduce the concept of mobile laboratories. This idea is already in existence but needs to be put into better practice.

(b) Science education through science kits is another point for consideration of the authorities. The DE learner who is opting for a science course may be supplied with a properly equipped science kit after he deposit some caution money.

(c) The facilities in study centres can be expanded to included science laboratories also.

Suggestions for Further Studies

1. The study of wastage and stagnation in DES in Andhra Pradesh.
2. A cost analysis of Distance Education provided by open university and School of Distance Education.
3. Learner response to use of multi-media in DES.
   Ex. Tele conference, radio broad casting etc.
4. Learner needs and re-designing of courses.
5. Attitudes of un-employed learners towards Distance Education System.
6. Attitudes of working women towards Distance Education System.
7. Qualitative analysis of self instructional materials in the Distance Education System.
8. Life goals cherished by Distance learners.
9. Job preferences of Distance Education learners.

It is the belief of the investigator that, the above studies can help in gathering data needed for an alround improvement of Distance Education System in the state.

Summary of Research

Providing proper Higher Education (HE) is of paramount importance to a developing country moving into the twenty-first century. Higher education provides and supplies a wide range of sophisticated manpower needed for the development of a nation. While intending to cater to the developmental needs of the society and of individuals, the higher education system aspires for practising democratic norms. It is expected that the system must be accessible to an optimum level of those citizens who are capable of pursuing higher studies.

Owing to certain inherent limitations, the formal system cannot act as a viable means for higher studies of those who are capable enough to study but belonged to the regions far away from the institutions, lacked motivation to continue with formal stream, belonged to upper age group, took employment at the end of schooling, found the formal system expensive and discontinued for one or other reasons, and could not take up the opportunity to pursue education as youngsters do etc. These limitations inherent in the formal system paved the way for the encouragement of parallel streams of higher education.

The open learning system has been initiated to augment opportunities for higher education, as an instrument of democratising education, and to make it a life long process. The flexibility and innovativeness of the open learning system are particularly suited to the diverse requirements of the citizens of India, including those who had joined the vocational stream.

In a developing country like India, Distance Education is well suited to meet the increasing needs and aspirations of clientele in higher education. As evidence the Distance Education Institutions (DEI) in India i.e., Open Universities and the institutes of Distance Education of conventional universities accounted for about 11.5 per cent of the enrolment in higher education in 1989-90. The share and role of Distance Education in catering to higher education is highly significant and is likely to increase in the coming decades.

Distance Education has been developing in a marvelously diverse fashion around the world.

The International Council for Distance Education (ICDE) has estimated that currently over 10 million students are taking degree courses at a distance, in the world.

There are now more that 35 Distance Education and Seven Open Universities in India i.e., (One National Open University, at Delhi, IGNOU and one each in the states of Andhra Pradesh, Maharashtra, Rajasthan, Bihar, Madhya Pradesh and Karnataka.

The DES is trying to share the task of providing higher education along with the conventional university system which was mainly vested with the responsibility of providing higher education in India.

Whether the DES is called an alternative channel or parallel stream for providing higher education, the fact to be acknowledged is, that Distance Education approach is attracting more and more learners every year. The Distance Education is a part of the present educational scene in India.

Currently in the State of Andhra Pradesh there is one Open University and five Distance Education centres functioning for the provision of higher education along with seven conventional universities.

The total enrolment of Distance Education students in India for the year 1989-1990 was 5.35 millions out of which the share of Andhra Pradesh was around 82,000.

Region-wise the southern region of India comprising of Andhra Pradesh, Karnataka, Kerala and Tamil Nadu states cater to 61.7 per cent of Distance Education Learners. Though Tamil Nadu is leading in the field of Distance Education in India, the enrolment figures show that the state of Andhra Pradesh ranks second during 1989-90.

Significance

The clientele to Distance Education stream of higher education in Andhra Pradesh is being catered to by one open university and five directorates attached to the conventional universities. The SDE, Andhra University and BRAOU are the oldest Distance Education agencies in the state.

The DES in Andhra Pradesh is in different stages of development. There is increasing enrolment and increased financial inputs into the system. In this context, the role of Distance Education in Andhra Pradesh in achieving the goals of higher education has significance.

The role of Distance Education in catering to the goals of higher education is unquestionable. The question that educationists have to answer is, how best to improve the Distance Education machinery to cater to the changing goals of higher education. Quantitative expansion by itself is not an indication of quality education.

The DES if it has to properly cater to higher education, has also to take care of the defects and move in the direction of realising the goals of higher education, as projected by New Education Policy (1986).

The National Policy of Education (1986) which has recognised and speltout the goals of higher education, while pointing out that higher education should be made dynamic, says.

The main feature of the programmes and strategies to impart necessary dynamism to the higher education system consist of the following:

1. Consolidation and expansion of institutions.
2. Development of autonomous colleges and departments.
3. Re-designing the courses.
4. Training of Teachers.
5. Strengthening of research.
6. Improvements in efficiency.
7. Creation of structures for co-ordination at the state and the national level.
8. Mobility.

While the growth of higher education through conventional universities has been steady and planned, the growth of higher education in India through Distance Education system is need based and fast developing. By virtue of the fact that Distance Education is attracting more and more students, a quantitative growth of this system in India is to be expected.

Mere quantitative expansion of the system cannot be an indicator of the quality of education. When the learners are limited in number, no doubt, the system is effective. But, the pressures of catering to increased number of learners like providing varied courses, providing Students Supports Services (SSS), maintaining timely learner contact by using multimedia, evolving higher quality self learning instructional materials (SLIMS) etc.; are needed to make this system effective. Then only, the goals of higher education can be realised, quality improved and the DE system can be made effective.

A system is effective, when it is running smoothly. From the view point of the learner the Distance Education system is to be effective and his entry into Distance Education stream made easy, the learning system has to be suitable to him, the administrative procedures like submitting applications, getting information, writing examinations, and passing out of the stream have to be planned, easy and least trouble some.

The system can be said to be effective when the organisational hierarchy is well defined, and each individual participating in the system has a favourable view of the concept. In the DES this favourable attitude is specially necessary for those at the helm of affairs.

The system will be effective, when the general trends are upward, like enrolment growth, economic growth, curriculum growth, and faculty growth.

Not many of the investigations have focussed proper attention on the area of the effectiveness of DES in realising the goals of higher education. Research into this area can influence planning, identification of defects, qualitative improvement of this system, need for restructuring the educational goals to suit the Distance Education learners and identification of the developing trends in the system.

Need for the Study

There is a need for studies in the area of the Effectiveness of DES in Realising the Goals of Higher Education.

It was felt that the holistic model of investigation to look at the intricate relationships will yield useful knowledge. There is a need to undertake evaluation studies of DES taking into account the context of the functioning of the system. This may help in giving directions for innovations in the DES in the Indian context.

Though, we speak of two systems by calling them distance and conventional; it should be remembered that, the learners of both the systems are aiming at higher education. Hence, evaluative studies of DES are as important as evaluative studies of the conventional system.

Almost every conventional university is equipped with a Distance Education Centre offering a wide range of courses. The number of Distance Education Centres in India at present are more that thirty five.

The quantitative growth in DES and its parallel growth as an alternative to conventional university education makes it the current area of educational research. There is a need for continuous comprehensive and periodic evaluation of its effectiveness.

The DES has developed a structural and organisational pattern of its own.

The DES in the modern world is considered the educational system of the future.

The state of Andhra Pradesh has become one of the pioneers and leaders in the field of Distance Education in India. The State Government and the Central Government are the funding agencies of this system. The system is expected to be effective in functioning by catering to the needs of a large and growing number of Distance Learners. Though the students composition of this system is different from that of a conventional university for higher education, research has shown that the Distance Education learner is equally motivated to receive higher education.

Evidently, both the systems should function effectively to realise the goals of higher education. It also means that recommendations made for improving the quality of higher education are applicable to both the systems. The recommendations of NPE (1986) for improving the quality of higher education in India, and the areas identified by them for strengthening the system have equal relevance to DES.

This piece of research is attempted with the following question which has educational implications to the state of Andhra Pradesh.

Is the Distance Education System in Andhra Pradesh effective to realise the goals of higher education?

Focus of the Study

Evaluative studies in Distance Education can be in terms of a region, nation or nations. To conduct this study viz., effectiveness of Distance Education system of Andhra Pradesh in realising the goals of higher education, descriptive survey method was adopted. Institutional studies within in the system are considered adequate to yield the desired information in the goals of the study.

For the purpose of this study, statistical information on Distance Education was chosen to the extent available.

It was felt desirable to focus the attention by adopting a three-way approach of data gathering viz., Tend analysis, Interviewing teachers, and gathering learner opinions, which will enable in drawing pertinent and useful conclusions. The focus was on the institution as a whole, and on the teachers and learners, in particular.

A study of well established Distance Education institutions in the state can help in drawing conclusions, which are applicable to the growing institutions. A systematic and well focussed understanding of the growth of two well established institutions, one Open University and the other SDE, can help in answering the research question. The institutions are to be studied using descriptive study approach in terms of growth and development, current status and anticipated future.

Hence, the main focus of this investigation is to draw generalizations about the effectiveness of Distance Education System in Andhra Pradesh by studying and evaluating some well established institutions of the state.

The title of this study is

"EFFECTIVENESS OF DISTANCE EDUCATION SYSTEM OF ANDHRA PRADESH IN REALISING THE GOALS OF HIGHER EDUCATION — AN EVALUATION STUDY".

Objectives

The main aim of this investigation is to study effectiveness of the present Distance Education System in Andhra Pradesh in realising the goals of higher education. It is proposed to draw conclusions regarding the effectiveness.

A. Through Institutional Study by Identifying

1. Enrolment trends.
2. Economic trends.
3. Growth in infrastructure.
4. Curriculum and course trends.
5. The trend of learners success in the system.
6. Multi-media usage trends.

B. Through Faculty by

1. Identifying the faculty opinions on the goals of higher education that are realised by the Distance Education system.
2. Finding faculty opinions on areas of Distance Education system that need to be improved and strengthened.

C. Through Learners by

1. Identifying the learner opinion a the goals of higher education that are realised by the Distance Education system.
2. To identify the major learner opinions towards the Distance Education system.
3. Finding learner opinion a areas of Distance Education system that need to be improved and strengthened.

The present study of Distance Education was made with the above objectives in mind.

Review of Related Literature

Most of the investigations on DE in India are at micro level, piece meal, informative and did not take into account the context of the overall functioning of the system. The investigations have also not focussed on the qualitative aspects, of the performance of the students of the two system viz., Distance Education and conventional. Some of them emphasised the holistic model of investigation, looking at the intricate relationship of influential factors, in single institutional programmes. It points out the med for making attempts at studying the Distance Education System of a region as a whole. There is also a need for evaluating the effectiveness of DES in Indian context.

Method of Investigation

The investigation was taken up with the promise that the role of Distance Education in catering to the goals of higher education in unquestionable.

The main focus of this piece of research work was to find out whether Distance Education System in Andhra Pradesh is effective to realise goals of higher education.

Selection of Institutions for the Study

The School of Distance Education (SDE) of Andhra University, affiliated to a conventional University and BRAOU which was started by Government of Andhra Pradesh, in line with policy on Distance Education in India are the two oldest Distance Education institutions of the state. They represent the Distance Education system in Andhra Pradesh. Hence, these two institutions were selected.

Method and Design of the Study

This study comes under descriptive research and adopts a combination of trend analysis and survey approach. The major objective of this study was to evaluate the effectiveness of the Distance Education System in realising the goals of higher education in Andhra Pradesh. It was proposed to answer the research question by :

(a) Identifying and evaluating the growth trends in Distance Education System in Andhra Pradesh.

(b) Identifying the areas in this system that need to be strengthened and evaluation its effectiveness in goal realisation with the help of the above data.

Conclusions are drawn by studying the selected representative institutions of the Distance Education System in Andhra Pradesh.

Design of the Study

Topic : Effectiveness of Distance Education System in Andhra Pradesh for Realising Goals of Higher Education.

Research Method Chosen : Descriptive Method — Trend Analysis and Survey

Institution : 1. School of Distance Education
Andhra University
Vishakhapatnam

2. BRAOU, Hyderabad

Sl. No.	*Purpose*	*Sources of Data*	*Instruments Used*	*Sample and Selection Procedure*	*Data Collection Procedures*	*Analysis of Data*
1.	Opinions about Goal Realisation Through Distance education System in Andhra Pradesh	(a) Faculty	Interview schedule	30 Purposive Sampling	Interview	Descriptive and Summarisation
		(a) Learners	Opinionnaire 3 point scale	400 Quota Sampling	Administration of Opinionnaire	Frequency counting percentage
2.	Identifying areas of Distance Education System that need strengthening	(a) Faculty	Interview schedule	30 Purposive Sampling	Interview	Descriptive and Summarisation
		(a) Learners	Opinionnaire 3 point scale	400 Quota Sampling	Administration of Opinionnaire	Frequency Counting Percentage
3.	Growth Trends	Official records Annual reports Evaluation reports	Preparing Statistical table from available sources	Office records of BRAOU and SDE	Observation	Descriptive analysis of growth trends.

Construction of Tools

I. Interview Schedule for Faculty Members

An open ended interview schedule was prepared.

The interview schedule for the faculty members was prepared, mainly keeping view the areas of higher education that need to be strengthened.

II. Construction of Opinionnaire for the Learners

After reviewing the related literature, and discussions with colleagues and experts in the field of higher education, an opinionnaire was prepared to ascertain the opinions of learners on the effectiveness of Distance Education in realising the goals of higher education.

Opinions was gathered from the students of Distance Education System by asking them to evaluate the Distance Education System with reference to the following aspects.

(a) Overall facilities in the system.

(b) Courses, curriculum and evaluation.

(c) Student support services like :

  (i) Assignments, Course material, Study Centres,

  (ii) Personal Contact Programme,

  (iii) Counselling,

  (iv) Multi-media.

(d) Difficulties faced by the students in the system.

(e) Students were also asked to give their opinions about the goals of H.E, that are being realised by the Distance Education System.

Trend Analysis

The purpose of trend analysis in this study is to analyse data from two types of distance education institutions namely BRAOU and School of Distance Education of Andhra University, in terms of selected institutional growth parameters. The parameters chosen were:

1. Student enrolment.

2. Income and expenditure growth.
3. Successful course completion by students.
4. Growth in number of discipline.
5. Growth in research
6. Growth in study centres.
7. Growth in use of multi-media.

From available sources in the institutions the data for trend analysis was gathered, The investigator used the documents from the two institutions to develop the trend tables.

Sampling, Administration and Scoring of Tools

(a) *Interview Schedule*

The sample for the interviews was selected from, the faculty working in the academic head quarters of the two Distance Education Institutions. Fifteen faculty members from BRAOU, Hyderabad and fifteen from School of Distance Education, Visakhapatnam were contacted.

It was felt that this sample of faculty at the helm of affairs is a purposive sample, because they belong to the group of individuals involved in the process of planning, administering and evaluating the process of Distance Education. The interview data was recorded, consolidated and verbally analysed.

(b) *Opinionnaire of Learners*

It was opined that securing a proper representative sample of learners of Distance Education System is possible by applying the principle of Quota sampling to the available information. The coursewise enrolment figures for the two Distance Education Institutions for the year 1995-96 could be secured.

The Opinionnaire was administered on total sample of 400 Distance Education students studying in Andhra Pradesh Open University and school of Distance Education. Each sub-sample was of the size of 200.

Since, three point scale was adopted, the frequency of response was arrived at for each statement. For convenience of interpretation, the frequencies are converted into percentages. The data is reported as percentages,

Findings and Discussions

The reference points for evaluating the DE system were:

— Its effectiveness in realising the goals of higher education as viewed by faculty and learners.

— Overall areas that need strengthening, in terms of National Policy of Education (1986) recommendations, as identified by faculty.

— The existing strengths and weakness of the system as viewed and identified by the learner.

On the basis of the finding, it is concluded that the DES is functioning effectively to the state of Andhra Pradesh.

As evident from the faculty and learner opinions, the system is providing to the realisation of the knowledge objective, helping the learners to understand social issues, and enabling these to contribute to national development. It is also evident that the Distance Education approach is providing teachers for the educational system.

The DES in Andhra Pradesh is showing healthy growth trends as was evident from the findings of the trend data. The system is economically sound. Student expenditure per year is satisfactory. The system has the necessary infrastructure facilities.

There is a gradual increases of student enrolment in this system. The DES evidently has the capacity to handle large student populations. This can be seen from the current annual enrolment of nearly 45,000 in each of the institutes studied. The administrators of Distance Education have the plans and confidence to handle even higher student enrolments of up to 75,000 in each institution in future. The trends of the demand for enrolment indicate that in the coming ten years the student enrolment into the DES is likely to increase two fold.

Evidently, the DES is playing its effective role in field of womens' education. Nearly thirty per cent of the Distance Education learners are women students. From the view point of flexibility and accessibility the DES has gone closer and closer to the learners, as nearly seventy per cent of those that want to enter the Distance Education stream of higher education are choosing the non-formal entry route.

In line with the National Policy of Education that the medium of instruction is to be in mother tongue, the DES is ale to cater to the students who want the other tongue as the medium of learning. As a matter of fact, eighty per cent of the Distance Education learners are receiving education in their mother tongue i.e.,Telugu.

The DES is offering a number of courses in various disciplines. The courses offered range from the foundation courses to research degrees. There is a gradual growth in the number of courses being offered by the DES. At present, DES has also recognised the need for providing vocational courses, short duration diploma courses, and is offering these courses in areas like Library science, Business Management, Nutrition etc.

The DES is also contributing much in the area of research. The faculty at the helm of affairs is highly qualified and willing to take up the research function also.

There is a steady growth in the number of study centres. As part of the Student Support Services, the study centres are playing a key role in the DES.

Like any other modern educational system, the Distance Education approach also has to depend on multi-media. Compared to the earlier years, now a days DES in A.P., is giving increased emphasis to the use of multi-media. Attempts are being made to liberally use television net works and radio broad casting. The system is producing some audio, and video cassettes for the use of learners. But, it is observed in this study that the systematic usage of multi-media in the DES is not evidently viewed by the producers and consumers.

The system is efficiently producing and supplying the study materials to the learners. The study material is following the pattern of self instructional material with inbuilt self evaluation approach.

But, the trends in overall, success rate of students of DES need detailed and thorough investigation. In every educational system there is wastage and stagnation. DES is no exception to this. The overall trends in results indicate that the success rate of the students is low. Between seven to fifteen per cent of the students are passing out successfully.

The student profile shows, that nearly seventy per cent a e opting for Bachelor of Arts degree in Telugu medium. As already reported, nearly seventy per cent of the students are entering through non-formal stream. This is a large chunk of the student population in the DES and, may be, it is the reason why the results are dismal.

This investigator strongly opines that wastage and stagnation studies on DES in Andhra Pradesh will serve a useful purpose to give guide-lines to make the system more effective.

The NPE (1986) has made various recommendations to strengthen the institutions of higher education. DES has evolved as a parallel approach to higher education by adopting the Distance mode of learning and, the inherent characteristics of flexibility and accessibility. System wise, a direct comparision of conventional higher educational system with the DES cannot be made. The Distance Education is latest innovation in the field of education. The clientele are all adults from different walks of life and self motivated. Of late, the Distance Education is serving more to the cause of higher education.

The faculty of the DES who are at the helm of affairs, expressed a range of opinions on what areas are to be strengthened.

One important observation was, that DES is an effective as the conventional system in realising the aims of higher education. This shows a confidence in themselves and confidence about he effectiveness of the system.

The system needs expansion and consolidation of facilities to meet the future demands for higher education. The DES requires modernisation of the curricula to meet the growing demands of specialisation. There is a need for redesigning of the courses. Substantiating the faculty opinions, this also evident in view of the limited number of conventional degrees that are being offered by the system. There is also a demand for job-oriented courses from learners.

More than autonomy, what the system needs is better co-ordination. Need for autonomy was not expressed by the faculty. The DES needs an apex body to monitor and co-ordinate the system. This is necessary in view of the need for uniform curricula, uniform courses, and common rules and regulations.

The learners experience in this education system was another reference point for evaluating its effectiveness.

The learners of DES in A.P., make the following position assessment. From their view point:

1. The system is accessible.
2. Infrastructure facilities are adequate.
3. Courses are suitable to the present needs.
4. Good teacher-student report exists.
5. Personal contact programmes are useful.
6. Good counselling is given.
7. The learner requirements are:
   (a) More number of courses with job-orientation are needed.
   (b) Improvement in evaluation procedures is desirable.
   (c) The learner problems are :
      (i) Difficulty is there with regard to the availability of library books.
      (ii) Difficulty in receiving information about examination dates and results is felt.

The learner evaluated the effectiveness of DES is realising the goals of higher education as follows:

1. The system is helping in understanding social issues.
2. The system is contributing for national development.
3. The system is able to prepare teachers needed by educational system in India.
4. The system is not effective in helping them to develop specialised acknowledge.

Suggestions

The following suggestions may be considered to make the DES more effective.

1. Regionwise surveys of needs of learners aspiring to enter into the DES will result in useful data to plan job-oriented courses.

2. Each institution in the DES is adopting its won multi-media approach. Common multi-media packages for use of the Distance Education learners, irrespective of the institution in which they are studying, will serve and useful purpose.
3. Each institution must make a honest and detailed study of wastage and stagnation. This wastage and stagnation data may be taken as the basis for SSS, PCP and other important aspect. This data will be very helpful in planning to make the Distance Education approach more effective.
4. An apex body to monitor DES is extremely desirable and urgently needed.
5. The DES is mainly self-funding. Of late, it is receiving substantial grants and funds from UGC and the State Government. In the conventional system, there are certain provisions for the students community on the basis of the reservations and economic status. The extension of a similar facility to the student of Distance Education will serve a useful purpose of social justice in Indian context.
6. Development of a holistic model for evaluating the effectiveness of DES periodically is needed. This type of model can be diagnostic in nature. It can enable the authorities to implement the recommendations which will be specific and concrete. The evaluation programme has to evolve simple and well defined tools.

The type of tools that can be used here are:

(a) Institutional environment.
(b) System co-ordination.
(c) Attitudes of faculty and learners.
(d) Growth trends in the system.
(e) Basic cost analysis.
(f) Public opinion.

A team of trained objective investigators can be made to conduct this type of educational audit every year, make recommendations for improving system efficiency and bring out a generalised picture of the effectiveness of the system from time to time. This kind of continuous cross sectional studies can be subjected to meta analysis for validity of the recommendations.

7. Science education through Distance Mode appears to be weak in the DES of Andhra Pradesh. No doubt social sciences are much preferred by the DE learners and there is a heavy demand for arts courses. In order, to meet the demand for science education through DE approach, some improvements are necessary.

Teaching of science needs well equipped laboratories. The conventional universities and degree colleges have well organised laboratories meant for teaching and research programmes. But the DE Institutions in Andhra Pradesh are still in the stage of organising themselves for teaching science.

Keeping in view, the limitations of Distance learners, the following suggestions to improve science education for DES are made.

(a) Since the learner cannot come to the institution quite often, there is a need to introduce the concept of mobile laboratories. This idea is already in existence but needs to be put into better practice.

(b) Science education through science kits is another point for consideration of the authorities. The DE learner who is opting for a science course may be supplied with a properly equipped science kit after he deposits some caution money.

(c) The facilities in study centres can be expanded to include science laboratories also.

Suggestions for Further Studies

1. The study of wastage and stagnation in DES in Andhra Pradesh.

2. A cost analysis of Distance Education provided by open university and School of Distance Education.

3. Learner response to use of multi-media in DES.
   Ex. Tele conference, radio broad casting etc.

4. Learner needs and re-designing of courses.

5. Attitudes of un-employed learners towards Distance Education System.

6. Attitudes of working women towards Distance Education System.

7. Qualitative analysis of self instructional materials in the Distance Education System.

8. Life goals cherished by Distance learners.

9. Job preferences of Distance Education learners.

It is the belief of the investigator that, the above studies can help in gathering data needed for an alround improvement of Distance Education System in the state.

Bibliography

Aggarwal, J.C., (1992), *Education Policy in Indian Retrospect and Prospect*, Shipra Publication, New Delhi.

Aggarwal, J.C., (1993), *Development and Planning of Modern Education*, Vikas Publishing House Pvt. Ltd., New Delhi.

Aggarwal, J.C., (1983), *Land Marks in the History of Modern Indian Education*, Vikas Publishing House Pvt. Ltd., New Delhi.

Ahluwalia, S.P., Bais, H.S., (1992), *Education Issues and Challenges*, Ashish Publishing House, New Delhi, p. 36.

Annual Reports, Andhra University, Visakhapatnam 1987-88, 88-89, 89-90, 90-91, 91-92, 93-94, 95-96.

A profile, (1995), Audio video production and rsearech centre BRAOU, Hyderabad.

Asia and the Pacific, (1992), *A Survey of Distance Education*, Vol-I, UNESCO.

Bala Subramanium, S., (1976), *The Status of Correspondence Courses in India*, University News.

Bates, T., (1962), *Trends in the use of A.V. Media in Distance Education System*, Athabasca University, ICCE, Edmonton.

Beardsley, *(1975), The free University of Iran*, in Mackenzie, N., et al.,(ed.), Open Learning, Paris, UNESCO Press.

Best, J.W., and James, V., Kahn., (1986), *Research in Education Fifth Edition*, Prentice-Hall of India, Private Ltd., New Delhi.

Bhaskara, Rao. D., (1996), *National Policy on Education*, Vol-2, Anmol Publications Pvt. Ltd., New Delhi.

Bhaskara, Rao. P., 1986, *IGNOU — System and Communication* - National Conference on Distance Education, Gujarat University, Ahmedabad.

Biswal, B.N., (1978), *A Study of Correspondence Education in Indian Universities*, An unpublished Ph.D. Thesis, CASE, M.S. University, Baroda.

Borje, Holmberg, (1997), *Distance — Education Theory Again Open Learning*, The Journal of Open and Distance Learning, Vol.12 (1), p. 31, Pitman Publishing.

Buch, M.B., (197), (ed.), *Third Survey of Research in Education*, NCERT, New Delhi.

Buch, M.B., (1991), (Ed.), *Fourth Survey of Research in Education* 1983-88, Vol. II, NCERT, New Delhi.

Budget Estimates, 1987-1993 and1994-1997, Andhra University, Visakhapatnam.

Chambers, E.A., (1992), *Workload and the Quality of Student Learning*, Studies in Higher Education 17(2), p. 141-153.

Childs, O.D., (1971), *Recent Research Developments in Correspondence Education*, In Mackene and Chistansen (eds.), The Changing World of Correspondence Study : International Readings. Pennylvania State University Press.

Crooks, Beryl, (1987), *Indicators of Performance at the Open University with Particular Reference to Teaching*, The Open University, Milton Keynes, U.K.

Das, Mamata, (1991), *Approaches to Learning and Academic Performance of Students in Open and Traditional Universities.* A Doctoral Thesis, Ph.D. Jawaharlal Nehru University, New Delhi.

Deshmukh, K.G., (1986), *Gensis and the Growth of Distance Education*, University News, Special Issue Aiu, Publication, November 8.

DE-1., *Growth and Philosophy of Distance Education, History and Present Status*, IGNOU Course Material (DE-1, 1987) Division of Distance Education, New Delhi

DE-1., *Growth and Philosophy of Distance Education, Growth and Present Status*, IGNOU Course Material (DE-1, 1987) Division of Distance Education, January, New Delhi.

Distance Education Research in Centre for Evaluation (1991) *A Review*, BRAOU, Hyrerabad.

Distance Education in Asia and the Pacific, (1993), Country Papers - Volume I, UNESCO.

Dutt., (1976), *Correspondence Courses in India,* Winged Words, University of Delhi.

Education in Asia, (1996), *Open University and Distance Education,* Quarterly Journal Ministry of HRD Government of India. Vol. VI, July-August-September.

Entwistle., and Ramsden, (1983), *Understanding Student Learning,* London : Croom Helm.

Erdos, Renee, F., (1957), *Teaching by Correspondence,* UNESCO Source Book, London, p. 2.

Escotat, M.S., (1980), *Tendencies de la Education Superior a Distancia,* San Jose Editoria UNED Cited in Rumble, G. and Harry, K. (eds., 1983), The Distance Teaching, London: Crobom Helm, p. 234.

Fair Bank, W.E., (1982), As Quoted in Wilbu Schram, *Some Notes on Distance Teaching,* The Asian Messenger Spring.

Feaseley, E., Charles., (1982), *Distance Education,* Encyclo Peaedia of Educational Research, Vol. I, The Free Press, London.

Garret, H.E., (1985), *Statistics in Psychology and Education,* Vakils, Feffer and Simons Ltd., Bombay.

Gilbert, D.D., Mounts, T.D., and Frost, A.A., (1982), *Computer Graphics Simulation of Chemical Instrumentation, Absorption Spectrophotometers,* Journal of Chemical Education 59: 661-663.

Glatter, R., Wedell, E.O., (1971), *Study by Correspondence,* London, Longman.

Graham, A.C., (1971), *What Hermods Students Think of Assignments,* in Correspondence Education in Hermods, Fack Malmo 70, Sweden.

Greenberg, Elinor, (1980), *The University Without Walls,* (UWW) Programme at Loutto Heights College : Individualisation for adults, New Directions for Higher Education 8(1).

Hand Book — 1993-94, BRAOU, Hyderabad.

Holmberg, B., (1977), *Distance Education,* Kegan Paul, London.

Holmberg, B., (1985), *Status and Trends of Distance Education,* Lector

Publishing House, p.142.

Indian Higher Education, *Policies and Plans* - ES 301, (1991), IGNOU Course Material.

Indira Gandhi National Open University, *Project Report*, 1985, Educational Consultants India Limited, (A Government of India Enterprise) New Delhi.

Jose Chander, N., (1987), *Open Learning System the Concept*, India International Centre Seminar on Open Learning System : Concept and Future.

Keegan, D., and Rumble., (1982), *The Distance Teaching At. University Level*, Edt., by Rumble and Horry St. Martin's Press, New York.

Keegan, D., (1986), *The Foundation of Distance Education*, Croom Helm London.

Keegan, D., (1990), *Foundations of Distance Education*, Second Edition, London, Rout ledge.

Kaye, A., and Rumble, G., (1981), *Distance Teaching for Higher and Adult Education*, London, Croom Helm.

Khan, I., (1982), *Suitability of Teaching English Through Correspondence Courses as Offered by some Indian Universities at the First Degree Level*, Ph.D., Dissertation, Utkal University.

Koul, Lokesh, (1984), *Methods of Educational Research*, Vani Educational Books A division of Vikas Publishing Pvt. Ltd., New Delhi.

Lorenzo, Garia, Aretio, (1996), *Assessing Results in Distance Learning Centres*, Epistolo Didaktika, The European Journal of D.E., England, p. 44.

MC Intosh N.E., (1974), *The Open University Student*, in Tunstall, J. (ed.), The open University Opens, London Routledge and Keegan Paul.

Mohanty, J., (1993), *Dynamics of Higher Education in India* Deep & Deep Publications, New Delhi, p. 32.

Moore, M., (1977), *A Model of Independent Study*, EPISTOLODIDAKTIKA, 1977/1, 640.

National Policy on Education — 1986, Programme of Action, Ministry of Human Resource Development Government of India, August 1986.

National Policy on Education — 1986, Ministry of Human Resource Development, Government of India, New Delhi, 1986.

Neil, M., (1981), *Education of Adults at a Distance,* London, Kogan page.

Olugbemiro J. Jegede D.E., (1994), Research Priorities for Australia, *A Study of the Opinions of Distance Educators and Practioners,* Distance Education, Vol., 15, No. 2, Australia, p. 234.

Open University, 1978, *The Basic Ideas Sir Walter Perry,* The Open University Press.

Panda, S.K., and Panda, B.N., (1966), *Distance Education Social Status and Personality Adjustment,* Indian Education Review.

Pandey, S.K., (1980), *The Economics of Correspondence Education to Indian Universities,* An Unpublished Ph.D. Thesis, Meerut University, Meerut.

Paramaji, (1984), *Open University — a Conceptual Analysis* — Distance Education, Sterling Publishers, New Delhi.

Perry, W., (1976), *Open University A Personal Account,* by the First Vice Chancellor, Milton Keynes, The Open University Press.

Peters, O., (1965), *Der ternunterricht, Correspondence Teaching* Weinheim and Berlin, Verlag Julius Beltz.

Peter, O., (1971), *Texte Zum Hochschulfern Studium,* Weinheim, Beltz.

Pfeifer, J.W., (1971), *The Effect of Letters and Post Cards of Encouragement on the Submission of Lessons in Correspondence Study Courses,* Doctoral Dissertation, University of Lowa, Lowacity.

Pillai, J.K., and Mohan, S., (1983), *Impact and Performance of Madurai Kamaraj University,* Department of Education, Madurai Kamaraj University.

Powell, E., (1971), *Survey of Students Enrolled for Correspondence Instruction,* George Centre for Continuing Education, University of Georgia, Athens.

Pradhan, N., (1986), *University Education Access and Success* Education quarterly, Ministry of HRD, New Delhi.

Raghunath, K., (1994), *Management of Distance Education*, Ajantha Publications, Delhi.

Ramaiah, P., Subba Rao. C., and Srinivasacharyulu, G., (1991), *Trends in Distance Education* Research in BRAOU, Paper Presented at the Educational Technology Conference, Bhubaneswer, AIAET, December.

Ram Reddy, G., (1986), APOU: *Some Reflections, University,* News, Special Issue, National Conference on Distance Education.

Ram Reddy, G., (1983), *Distance Education in India, an Evaluation of Higher Distance Education Results*, Universidad De Nacional A Distancia, Madrid.

Ram Reddy. G., (1986), *The Indira Gandhi National Open University : Its role in Higher Education*, Journal of Higher Education, 11, 1-2.

Rathore, H.C.S., (1991), *A Critical Evaluation of the Systems Adopted for Management of Teaching and Learning in the Existing Correspondence Institutes in India,* New Delhi, A Project Report Submitted to NEAPA.

Report of the Indian Education Commission, 1964-66, (1970), NCERT, New Delhi.

Ronald, Gross., (1979), *Future Directions for Open Learning, A Report Based on an Invitational Conference on Open Learning Programmes,* U.S. Department of Health, Education and Welfare.

Sahoo.P.K., (1985), *A Study of Correspondence Education in an Indian University*, An Unpublished, Ph.D., Thesis, Case, M.S., University, Baroda.

Sahoo, P.K., (1991 b), *A Contextual and Comparative Analysis of Open Learning System with Distance Education and Formal Education*, Paper Submitted to Educational Technology Conference, BBSR, AIAET.

Sarwal, A., 1984, *Preparation of Teacher Training Correspondence Courses Units for English Language Teaching*, Unpublished M.Lit., Dissertation, CIEFL, Hyderabad.

Satyanarayana, M., and Jyothirmayee, Kidambi., (1995), *Students Enrolment in Undergraduate Programme,* A Study Centre for Evaluation, BRAOU, Hyderabad.

School of Correspondence Courses, (1995), *A Profile,* Andhra University Visakhapatnam.

School of Correspondence Courses, (1997), *A Status Report,* Submitted to the U.G.C. IX Plan Visiting Committee under the Convenorship of Prof. S. Acharya A.C., Visakhapatnam.

Schuyer, E.H., (1981), *The Open University in the Netherlands.,* Higher Education and Research in Netherlands, C 1/2; Winterspring, 3-11.

Sesha Ratnam, C., (1994), *Multi-Media Package in Open Learning System,* Ph.D., Thesis, Osmania University, Hyderabad.

Sharma, K., and Bhushan, A., 1976, *Systems Approach to Contact Programme in Correspondence Education Situation,* IUA for Continuing Education, New Delhi.

Short, L.N., (1967), *The Educational and Administrative Problems of Part-Time Student,* in Proceedings of the Inter University Conference on Part-Time Teaching in Australian Universities, University of Queensland, Brisbane.

Sims, Ripley, S., (1978), *New Trends in Correspondence Education,* Paper Offered in the report of the 11th World Conference held in Delhi.

Singh, Amrik., (1987), *How to Train Teachers : A Role for the Open University,* India International Centre Seminar on Open Learning System : Concept and Future.

Singh, Bakhshish, (1987), *Open Teaching - Learning System and the Indian Scenario,* India International Centres— Seminar on concept and future.

Singh, Sukhdev, (1977), *Teaching by Correspondence in India,* Light and light, Delhi.

Sivaswaroop, Pathaneni, (1996), *An Assessment of Motivation of Distance Learners,* A Case Study Indian Journal of Open Learning, V. 5. No. 1, IGNOU, New Delhi, January, .p. 9.

Sloan, D., (1966), *Survey Study of University Correspondence Drop-outs and Cancellations in the Home Study*, Review, Vol. 7. No. 3 Fall.

Sponder, B.M., (1991), *Distance Education in Rural Alaska : As Overview of Teaching and Learning Practices in Audio Conference Courses*, (2nd edn.), A.K. Fairbank, University of Alaska, Fairbanks Centre for Cross Cultural Studies.

Srinivasacharyulu, G., and Ramaiah, P., (1994), *Funding of Distance Education : A Case study of an Open University*, Indian Journal of Open Learning Vol. 3 No. 1 pp. 41-44 , January, 1994.

Sujatha, K., (1988), *Research on Distance Education in India*, Indian Journal of Distance Education 2.

Towards an Open Learning System, (1991), Report of the Committee on the Establishment of an Open University, A.P., Hyderabad.

Tunstall, Jeremy, (ed.), 1974, *The Open University Opens*, London, Routledge Keegan Paul.

UGC, *Report for the Year*, 1982-83, UGC, New Delhi 1983.

University Education Commission Report , 1948-49, Government of India, Delhi.

Venkaiah, V., (1996), *Management Education in Open University System: Role of Educational Technology*, Synergy - Facets of Research in Open Learning, O.K. Fine Arts Press (P.) Ltd., Delhi.

Vydehi, M., (1984), *A Critical Evaluation of the Distance Teaching Materials Leading to a Reformed Instructional Format for these Materials*, Unpublished M. Lit., Dissertation , CIEFL, Hyderabad.

Wiegers, K.E., and Smith,. S.G., (1980), *The use of Computer Based Chemistry Lessons in the Organic Laboratory Courses*, Journal of Chemical Education.

Wilson, S.J.M., (1980), *Experimental Simulation in the Undergraduate Physical Laboratory*, American Journal of Physics, 48: 701-704.

Willingham, J., (1971), *A Correspondence Tutorial Method of Teaching Freshmen College Composition*, University Extension, University of Kansas, Lawrence, Kansas, Quoted in

Machenzie, O., and Christensen, E.L., (ed.), the Changing World of Correspondence Study, London. The Pennsylvania Sate University Press.

World of Learning, Thirty Sixth Edition, (1986), Europe Publications Ltd.

Zachariah, A., Natu, M.V. Singh.D., and Singh.T., (1993), *Students Perceptions of the Curriculum and Teaching Methodology for MBBS Course*, Indian Journal or Medical Education.

APPENDIX— I

INTERVIEW SCHEDULE FOR FACULTY MEMBERS OF DISTANCE EDUCATION

1. Do you think that Distance Education System in the state is helping in realisation of the goals of higher education? why? How?
2. Do you think that there is a need for expansion of Distance Education Institutions in the State?
3. Do you feel that the academic faculties in Distance Education System have enough autonomy? Why?
4. Do you think that there is a need for redesigning the courses in Distance Education System?
5. Do you think that the Distance Education is playing a role in producing and training teachers for the educational system?
6. What are your suggestions for strengthening research in the Distance Education System?
7. What are the areas of Distance Education System that need to be strengthened?

   (a) Improvement of facilities.

   (b) Study centres.

   (c) Personal contact programmes.

   (d) Use of multi-media.

   (e) Study of materials for learners.

8. Do you think that there is a need for national apex body to monitor the Distance Education system in our country/state?
9. Do you think that in distance Education System the learner has mobility?

   Ex: (a) Freedom to choose courses.

   (b) Rules and regulations.

   (c) Freedom to move from one institution to another institutions.

APPENDIX—II

OPINIONNAIRE FOR STUDENTS

Personal Data

Please give the following information:

1. Name:

2. Course Studying:

Instruction

Given below are the statements. Please read each statement carefully. To enable your to make your responses easily and quickly, a scale has been provided. Please encircle on the scale following each item the symbol which best indicates your opinion.

The symbols stand for the following:

A = Agree

U = Undecided

D = Disagree

AREA-I : Over all Facilities in Distance Education System

1. Distance Education Universities/Directorates are accessible to students in seeking information. A U D
2. The admission procedures are systematic. A U D
3. The facilities at study centres are very useful to students. A U D
4. The infrastructure facilities (Building, class rooms, library, P.C.P. Centres etc.) offer adequate accommodation. A U D

AREA-II : Curriculum, Courses, and Evaluation

1. There is a need to introduce more courses. A U D
2. There is a need for continuous evaluation in courses. A U D
3. Evaluation procedures should be improved. A U D
4. Courses are suitable to the needs of the students. A U D

5. More job oriented courses should be introduced. A U D
6. The Distance Education curriculum is very relevant to student needs. A U D
7. There is a need for introducing teacher education courses like B.Ed. A U D

AREA-III : Student Support Services (Course Material, Study Centres, Assignments, P.C.Ps. and Multi-media).

1. Course material is supplied in time. A U D
2. Course material is covering the entire syllabus. A U D
3. Assignment approach is properly followed. A U D
4. Assignment is given in terms of instructional goals. A U D
5. Study centres are quite useful. A U D
6. Counselling timings are suitable to students. A U D
7. The quality of counselling is satisfactory. A U D
8. Personal Contact Programmes (PCP) are beneficial to students. A U D
9. The teacher-student rapport during P.C.P. is encouraging. A U D
10. P.C.P. dates are convenient to students. A U D
11. Multi-media (Radio broadcast, audio cassettes, video cassettes and T.V.) are used effectively. A U D

AREA-IV: Realisation of the Goals of Higher Education

1. Distance Education (DE) approach helps in understanding social issues in the country. A U D
2. DE gives opportunity to understand economic issues in the country. A U D
3. DE enables understanding of cultural issues in the country. A U D
4. DE encourages the understanding of moral issues in the ccuntry. A U D

5. DE offers an understanding of the spiritual. A U D
issues in the country.
6. DE promotes the acquisition of specialised knowledge. A U D
7. DE develop specialised professional skills. A U D
8. DE helps to contribute to National Development. A U D
9. DE guides the students for teaching profession. A U D

AREA-V :

Aspects relating to difficulties faced by the Distance Education students.

Instructions

Given below are some items. Please read each item. To enable you to make your responses easily and quickly, a scale has been provided. Please encircle on the scale following each item to indicate your opinions. 'No Difficulty' 'Undecided' 'Difficulty'.

N = No difficulty.
U = Undecided.
D = Difficulty.

1. Admission procedures N U D
2. Payment of fees N U D
3. Eligibility certification N U D
4. Learning material N U D
5. Information about Personal Contact Programme N U D
6. Attending P.C.P. N U D
7. Library services N U D
8. Counselling N U D
9. Examination dates N U D
10. Publication of Examination results N U D

Index